# Step Forward

## Language for Everyday Life

**SERIES DIRECTOR**
### Jayme Adelson-Goldstein

Includes
Student Audio CD

## 2

### Ingrid Wisniewska

**OXFORD**
UNIVERSITY PRESS

# OXFORD
UNIVERSITY PRESS

198 Madison Avenue
New York, NY 10016 USA

Great Clarendon Street, Oxford OX2 6DP UK

Oxford University Press is a department of the University of Oxford.
It furthers the University's objective of excellence in research, scholarship,
and education by publishing worldwide in

Oxford  New York

Auckland  Cape Town  Dar es Salaam  Hong Kong  Karachi
Kuala Lumpur  Madrid  Melbourne  Mexico City  Nairobi
New Delhi  Shanghai  Taipei  Toronto

With offices in

Argentina  Austria  Brazil  Chile  Czech Republic  France  Greece
Guatemala  Hungary  Italy  Japan  Poland  Portugal  Singapore
South Korea  Switzerland  Thailand  Turkey  Ukraine  Vietnam

OXFORD and OXFORD ENGLISH are registered trademarks of
Oxford University Press

© Oxford University Press 2008

Database right Oxford University Press (maker)

Library of Congress Cataloging-in-Publication Data
Step Forward : English for everyday life.
    p. cm.
    Step Forward 1 by Jane Spigarelli;
    Step Forward 2 by Ingrid Wisniewska.
    ISBN: 978-0-19-439224-2 (1 : pbk.)
    ISBN: 978-0-19-439225-9 (2 : pbk.)
    1. English language--Textbooks for foreign students. 2. English
language--Problems, exercises, etc. I. Spigarelli, Jane  II. Wisniewska,
Ingrid.
    PE1128.S2143 2006
    428.2'4--dc22
                            2006040090

Executive Publisher: Janet Aitchison
Editorial Manager: Stephanie Karras
Editors: Margaret Brooks, Katie La Storia
Associate Editors: Melinda M. Beck, Olga Christopoulos
Art Director: Maj-Britt Hagsted
Senior Designer: Michael Steinhofer
Senior Art Editor: Judi DeSouter
Art Editor: Elizabeth Blomster
Manufacturing Manager: Shanta Persaud
Manufacturing Coordinator: Faye Wang

Student Book ISBN: 978 0 19 439225 9
Student Book with CD-ROM ISBN: 978 0 19 439654 7
Student Book as pack component ISBN: 978 0 19 439659 2
Audio CD-ROM as pack component ISBN: 978 0 19 439664 6

Printed in China

20  19  18  17  16

The publishers would also like to thank the following for their permission
to adapt copyrighted material:

p. 131 *Injury Facts*® 2004 Edition published by *National Safety Council*®

This book is printed on paper from certified and well-managed sources.

ACKNOWLEDGMENTS

*Cover photograph:* Corbis/Punchstock
*Back cover photograph:* Brian Rose

*Illustrations:* Ken Batelman p. 76, p. 101, p. 112, p. 113, p. 118 (ID cards); Annie
Bissett p. 3, p. 64 (phone bill), p. 117 (bus rules), p. 125; Dan Brown p. 41, p. 89;
Gary Ciccarelli p. 8, p. 102, p. 104 (people); Mark Collins p. 19 (season icons),
p. 69, p. 116; Laurie Conley p. 65, p. 137; Lyndall Culbertson p. 25, p. 49, p. 61,
p. 70, p. 80, p. 97, p. 102 (paint icons), p. 106, p. 115, p. 121, p. 122, p. 127
(emergency reports), p. 130, p. 141; Ken Dewar p. 77, p. 78, p. 78 (food), p. 79, p. 85,
p. 96 (first-aid kit), p. 133; Bill Dickson p. 56, p. 66, p. 114, p. 126; Jody Emery
p. 22, p. 36 (spots), p. 37, p. 94, p. 95, p. 145; Mike Hortens p. 19 (calendar),
p. 21, p. 32, p. 35, p. 48 (GED certificate), p. 91; Rod Hunt p. 29; Uldis Klavins p.
17, p. 53, p. 82, p. 127; Rose Lowry p. 24, p. 120, p. 142, p. 144; Karen Minot p.
40 (realia), p. 52 (realia), p. 100, p. 109, p. 140; Jay Montgomery p. 10, p. 90, p.
106, p. 118 (car); Derek Mueller p. 4, p. 16, p. 136, p. 138; Tom Newsom p. 40
(woman), p. 44; Terry Paczko p. 28, p. 58, p. 88; Karen Pritchett p. 5, p. 92; Jane
Spencer p. 6, p. 30, p. 42, p. 54, p. 128; Bryon Thompson p. 20, p. 27 (calendar),
p. 47, p. 71, p. 117 (signs), p. 131, p. 139; Eric Velasquez p. 124.

*Photographs:* Alamy: Robert Harding Picture Library Ltd., 144 (Niagara Falls); Jack
Alexander, 105 (CDs); Artiga Photo, 63 (office workers); Bill Bachmann,18 (multi-
cultural picnic); Janet Bailey, 58 (Asian female); Sky Bonillo, 12 (man at computer);
Brand X Pictures, 60 (office co-workers), 93 (injured soccer player); Myrleen Ferguson
Cale, 105 (books); Francesco Campani, 27 (man on cell phone); Jose Carillo, 18
(county fair); Comstock, 59, (woman typing), 26 (Chicago); Creatas, 15 (four adults),
57 (broken copier/woman); Bob Daemmrich, 143 (jogger); Kayte M. Deioma, 82
(older smiling woman); Mary Kate Denny, 46 (mail carrier); Judi DeSouter for OUP,
75 (sick man), 68 (man cleaning kitchen); Paddy Eckersley, 27 (woman on phone);
Getty Images: Photodisc, 12 (chef); Jeff Greenberg, 48 (veterinarian); Peter Griffith,
143 (football player, volleyball game); Tracy Hebden, 106 (socks); Noel Hendrickson,
68 (outdoor breakfast); Richard Hutchings, 105 (camera); Image 100, 87 (clerk and
customer); Image State: Andy Belcher, 141 (bungee jumper); Inmagine: Digital Vision,
12 (reading to child), 81 (chocolate), 82 (mature male); iStockPhoto.com: Andreas
Rodriguez, 108 (credit cards); Bonnie Kamin, 123 (police officer and motorist); Dennis
MacDonald, 132 (flood zone); Ricky John Malloy/Taxi, 57 (man with watermelons);
Felicia Martinez, 82 (grapes), 103 (area rug); Jupiter Images: Comstock 84 (fruit);
Masterfile: Tim Mantoani, 10 (four adult students); Michael Newman, 51 (interview),
70 (woman in office), 103 (lamp), 106 (sweater); John Neubauer, 144 (White House);
Omni Photo: Jeff Greenberg, 93 (injured cyclist), 144 (Grand Canyon); Shaun Parrin,
82 (soup can); Photodisc, 143 (basketball game); Photo Edit Inc.: Gary Conner, 2
(three adult students); Michael Newman, 99 (doctor's office); Susan Van Etten, 144
(Golden Gate Bridge); Photographers Direct: Richard Levine, 135 (blizzard); Photo
Network, 24 (cookout); PhotoObjects.net, 103 (paint cans); Punchstock: Corbis, 82
(Hispanic woman); Royalty Free Division, 12 (construction workers and family in
kitchen); Frank Siteman, 78 (Asian woman); Skjold Photographs, 111 (customer
service department); Steif & Schnare, 82 (sausages); Michael Steinhofer for OUP,
64 (man with bill); Stockbyte, 82 (yogurt), 103 (chair); Stockdisc Classic, 106
(tie); SuperStock: 130 (man on phone); Taxi, 52 (man on steps); 3 (Asian woman);
Thinkstock, 46 (car saleswoman); 58 (Indian male); Veer: Image 100, 82 (younger
woman); David Young-Wolff, 147 (movie theater), 18 (outdoor music festival), 34
(woman reading newspaper), 46 (accountant), 59 (man at computer), 72 (senior
center), 68 (jogger on phone).

We gratefully acknowledge the collaborative spirit,
commitment, and skill of the *Step Forward Book 2* editorial
and design team: Stephanie Karras, Meg Brooks, Melinda Beck,
Katie La Storia, Carla Mavrodin, Maj-Britt Hagsted,
Michael Steinhofer, and Lissy Blomster.
We also want to thank our students and colleagues who have
inspired us throughout this project.
**Ingrid Wisniewska**
**Jayme Adelson-Goldstein**

I would like to thank Jayme Adelson-Goldstein for her
inspiration and guidance throughout this book. I dedicate
this book to my husband Greg for his constant support
and encouragement.

-Ingrid

I thank Ingrid Wisniewska for her gentle but firm belief in
our students' ability to think for themselves, and I dedicate
this book to Meg Brooks: project manager, problem solver,
and free spirit.

-Jayme

*The Publisher and Series Director would like to acknowledge the following individuals for their invaluable input during the development of this series:*

**Vittoria Abbatte-Maghsoudi** Mount Diablo Unified School District, Loma Vista Adult Center, Concord, CA

**Karen Abell** Durham Technical Community College, Durham, NC

**Millicent Alexander** Los Angeles Unified School District, Huntington Park-Bell Community Adult School, Los Angeles, CA

**Diana Allen** Oakton Community College, Skokie, IL

**Bethany Bandera** Arlington Education and Employment Program, Arlington, VA

**Sandra Bergman** New York City Department of Education, New York, NY

**Chan Bostwick** Los Angeles Technology Center, Los Angeles, CA

**Diana Brady-Herndon** Napa Valley Adult School, Napa, CA

**Susen Broellos** Baldwin Park Unified School District, Baldwin Park, CA

**Carmen Carbajal** Mitchell Community College, Statesville, NC

**Jose Carmona** Daytona Beach Community College, Daytona Beach, FL

**Ingrid Caswell** Los Angeles Technology Center, Los Angeles, CA

**Joyce Clapp** Hayward Adult School, Hayward, CA

**Beverly deNicola** Capistrano Unified School District, San Juan Capistrano, CA

**Edward Ende** Miami Springs Adult Center, Miami Springs, FL

**Gayle Fagan** Harris County Department of Education, Houston, TX

**Richard Firsten** Lindsey Hopkins Technical Education Center, Miami, FL

**Elizabeth Fitzgerald** Hialeah Adult Center, Hialeah, FL

**Mary Ann Florez** Arlington Education and Employment Program, Arlington, VA

**Leslie Foster Davidson** Mitchell Community College, Statesville, NC

**Beverly Gandall** Santa Ana College School of Continuing Education, Santa Ana, CA

**Rodriguez Garner** Westchester Community College, Valhalla, NY

**Sally Gearhart** Santa Rosa Junior College, Santa Rosa, CA

**Norma Guzman** Baldwin Park Unified School District, Baldwin Park, CA

**Lori Howard** UC Berkeley, Education Extension, Berkeley, CA

**Phillip L. Johnson** Santa Ana College Centennial Education Center, Santa Ana, CA

**Kelley Keith** Mount Diablo Unified School District, Loma Vista Adult Center, Concord, CA

**Blanche Kellawon** Bronx Community College, Bronx, NY

**Keiko Kimura** Triton College, River Grove, IL

**Jody Kirkwood** ABC Adult School, Cerritos, CA

**Matthew Kogan** Evans Community Adult School, Los Angeles, CA

**Laurel Leonard** Napa Valley Adult School, Napa, CA

**Barbara Linek** Illinois Migrant Education Council, Plainfield, IL

**Alice Macondray** Neighborhood Centers Adult School, Oakland, CA

**Ronna Magy** Los Angeles Unified School District Central Office, Los Angeles, CA

**Jose Marlasca** South Area Adult Education, Melbourne, FL

**Laura Martin** Adult Learning Resource Center, Des Plaines, IL

**Judith Martin-Hall** Indian River Community College, Fort Pierce, FL

**Michael Mason** Mount Diablo Unified School District, Loma Vista Adult Center, Concord, CA

**Katherine McCaffery** Brewster Technical Center, Tampa, FL

**Cathleen McCargo** Arlington Education and Employment Program, Arlington, VA

**Todd McDonald** Hillsborough County Public Schools, Tampa, FL

**Rita McSorley** Northeast Independent School District, San Antonio, TX

**Gloria Melendrez** Evans Community Adult School, Los Angeles, CA

**Vicki Moore** El Monte-Rosemead Adult School, El Monte, CA

**Meg Morris** Mountain View Los Altos Adult Education District, Los Altos, CA

**Nieves Novoa** LaGuardia Community College, Long Island City, NY

**Jo Pamment** Haslett Public Schools, East Lansing, MI

**Liliana Quijada-Black** Irvington Learning Center, Houston, TX

**Ellen Quish** LaGuardia Community College, Long Island City, NY

**Mary Ray** Fairfax County Public Schools, Springfield, VA

**Tatiana Roganova** Hayward Adult School, Hayward, CA

**Nancy Rogenscky-Roda** Hialeah-Miami Lakes Adult Education and Community Center, Hialeah, FL

**Lorraine Romero** Houston Community College, Houston, TX

**Edilyn Samways** The English Center, Miami, FL

**Kathy Santopietro Weddel** Northern Colorado Literacy Program, Littleton, CO

**Dr. G. Santos** The English Center, Miami, FL

**Fran Schnall** City College of New York Literacy Program, New York, NY

**Mary Segovia** El Monte-Rosemead Adult School, El Monte, CA

**Edith Smith** City College of San Francisco, San Francisco, CA

**Alisa Takeuchi** Chapman Education Center, Garden Grove, CA

**Leslie Weaver** Fairfax County Public Schools, Falls Church, VA

**David Wexler** Napa Valley Adult School, Napa, CA

**Bartley P. Wilson** Northeast Independent School District, San Antonio, TX

**Emily Wonson** Hunter College, New York, NY

# TABLE OF CONTENTS

| Listening & Speaking | CASAS Life Skills Competencies | Standardized Student Syllabi/ LCPs | SCANS Competencies | EFF Content Standards |
|---|---|---|---|---|
| • Listen to the letters of the alphabet<br>• Greet, introduce, and say goodbye<br>• Ask and answer questions about a student ID<br>• Listen and say dates | 0.1.2, 0.1.4, 0.1.6, 2.3.2, 6.0.1, 6.0.2 | 39.01, 49.01, 49.02, 50.02 | • Listening<br>• Speaking<br>• Sociability | • Conveying ideas in writing<br>• Speaking so others can understand<br>• Listening actively |
| • Talk about personal learning styles and study strategies<br>• Listen for effective learning styles<br>• Listen for information during introductions<br>• Request clarification during introductions<br>• Talk about goals and make a plan<br><br>**Pronunciation:**<br>• Intonation during introductions | L1: 0.1.2, 0.1.5, 4.8.1, 7.2.5, 7.4.1, 7.4.5, 7.4.7, 7.4.9, 7.5.6<br>L2: 0.1.2, 0.1.5, 7.2.5, 7.4.1, 7.4.7, 7.4.9, 7.5.6<br>L3: 0.1.2<br>L4: 0.1.2, 0.1.4, 0.1.5, 6.0.3, 6.0.4, 6.1.4, 7.5.6<br>L5: 4.1.9, 7.1.1, 7.1.2, 7.1.3, 7.1.4, 7.2.5, 7.2.7, 7.5.1, 8.3.1, 8.3.2<br>RE: 0.1.2, 0.1.3, 1.1.4, 0.1.5, 0.2.4, 4.8.1, 7.2.6, 7.3.3, 7.4.7, 7.5.6 | L1: 49.10, 49.17<br>L2: 49.02, 49.06, 49.13, 49.16, 49.17<br>L3: 49.02, 49.16, 50.03, 50.08<br>L4: 49.16, 51.05<br>L5: 49.13, 49.16<br>RE: 49.17, 50.03 | Most SCANS are incorporated into this unit, with an emphasis on:<br>• Seeing things in the mind's eye<br>• Knowing how to learn<br>• Responsibility<br>• Self-management<br>• Participating as a member of a team | Most EFFs are incorporated into this unit, with an emphasis on:<br>• Observing critically<br>• Cooperating with others<br>• Using math to solve problems and communicate<br>• Reflecting and evaluating |
| • Talk about how weather affects feelings<br>• Listen for events and times on a calendar<br>• Discuss times and dates of events<br>• Ask and answer questions about future events<br>• Give, get, and clarify directions<br>• Talk about parties<br><br>**Pronunciation:**<br>• Stressed words when clarifying directions | L1: 0.1.2, 4.8.1, 7.4.5, 7.5.6<br>L2: 0.1.2, 0.1.5, 7.2.5, 7.5.1, 7.5.6<br>L3: 0.1.2, 0.1.5, 7.5.6<br>L4: 0.1.2, 0.1.5, 1.1.3, 6.0.3, 6.0.4, 6.3.3, 6.3.4, 6.6.6, 7.5.6<br>L5: 0.1.1, 0.1.5, 0.2.4, 1.9.4, 7.2.5, 7.4.7<br>RE: 0.1.3, 0.1.5, 1.9.4, 2.3.2, 2.6.3, 4.8.1, 7.2.6, 7.3.3 | L1: 39.03, 47.01, 49.02, 49.03, 49.10<br>L2: 42.01, 49.02, 49.13, 49.16, 50.06<br>L3: 49.01, 50.02<br>L4: 43.02, 49.02, 49.09, 49.16, 51.05<br>L5: 43.03, 49.16, 49.17<br>RE: 49.16, 49.17, 50.02, 50.06 | Most SCANS are incorporated into this unit, with an emphasis on:<br>• Seeing things in the mind's eye<br>• Knowing how to learn<br>• Responsibility<br>• Self-management<br>• Participating as a member of a team | Most EFFs are incorporated into this unit, with an emphasis on:<br>• Observing critically<br>• Using math to solve problems and communicate<br>• Cooperating with others<br>• Reflecting and evaluating |
| • Talk about household repairs<br>• Listen for features in a home<br>• Talk about features in your dream home<br>• Ask and listen for information about apartments<br>• Talk about U.S. population<br>• Talk about life in towns and cities<br><br>**Pronunciation:**<br>• Intonation of information and *Yes/No* questions | L1: 0.1.2, 0.1.5, 1.4.7, 1.7.5, 7.4.5, 7.5.6, 8.2.6<br>L2: 0.1.2, 0.1.5, 1.4.1, 1.4.2, 7.2.3, 7.4.7<br>L3: 0.1.2, 0.1.5, 1.4.1, 1.4.2, 7.2.3<br>L4: 0.1.2, 0.1.5, 1.4.2, 1.4.3, 6.0.3, 6.0.4, 6.1.3, 7.2.3<br>L5: 0.1.2, 0.1.5, 2.5.6, 7.2.5, 7.4.5, 7.4.7<br>RE: 0.1.2, 0.1.3, 0.1.5, 1.4.2, 4.8.1, 7.2.6, 7.3.3 | L1: 49.02, 49.10<br>L2: 45.07, 49.01, 49.02, 49.03, 49.13, 49.16, 49.17<br>L3: 45.07, 49.01, 49.16, 50.04<br>L4: 45.07, 49.02, 49.16, 51.05<br>L5: 40.01, 49.09, 49.16, 49.17<br>RE: 49.16 | Most SCANS are incorporated into this unit, with an emphasis on:<br>• Seeing things in the mind's eye<br>• Knowing how to learn<br>• Responsibility<br>• Self-management<br>• Interpreting and communicating information | Most EFFs are incorporated into this unit, with an emphasis on:<br>• Observing critically<br>• Using math to solve problems and communicate<br>• Cooperating with others<br>• Reflecting and evaluating |

| Listening & Speaking | CASAS Life Skills Competencies | Standardized Student Syllabi/ LCPs | SCANS Competencies | EFF Content Standards |
|---|---|---|---|---|
| • Talk about jobs, education, and work experience<br>• Listen for information about job ads<br>• Talk about jobs and required skills<br>• Ask and respond to interview questions<br>• Talk about jobs and educational opportunities<br>**Pronunciation:**<br>• Syllables in present and past verbs | **L1:** 0.1.2, 0.1.5, 4.1.6, 4.4.2, 7.4.5, 7.5.6<br>**L2:** 0.1.2, 0.1.3, 0.1.5, 4.1.5, 4.1.7<br>**L3:** 0.1.5, 0.2.4, 7.4.7<br>**L4:** 0.1.2, 0.1.3, 0.1.5, 0.2.1, 4.1.5, 4.1.7, 4.1.8, 4.4.2, 6.0.3, 6.0.4, 6.1.1<br>**L5:** 0.1.2, 2.5.6, 4.1.8, 4.1.9, 4.4.2, 4.4.5, 7.1.1, 7.1.2, 7.1.3, 7.2.5, 7.2.7, 7.4.5, 7.4.7<br>**RE:** 0.1.2, 0.1.3, 0.1.5, 4.8.1, 7.2.6, 7.3.3, 7.5.6 | **L1:** 35.01, 35.02, 35.05, 39.01, 49.02, 49.10<br>**L2:** 35.04, 35.06, 49.06, 49.13, 49.16<br>**L3:** 49.01, 49.16, 49.17, 50.02<br>**L4:** 35.06, 49.02, 49.16, 51.05<br>**L5:** 35.03, 40.01, 49.16, 49.17<br>**RE:** 49.16, 50.02 | Most SCANS are incorporated into this unit, with an emphasis on:<br>• Knowing how to learn<br>• Seeing things in the mind's eye<br>• Responsibility<br>• Self-management<br>• Interpreting and communicating information | Most EFFs are incorporated into this unit, with an emphasis on:<br>• Using math to solve problems and communicate<br>• Observing critically<br>• Cooperating with others<br>• Reflecting and evaluating |
| • Talk about workplace machines<br>• Listen for appropriate job behavior<br>• Talk about classroom rules<br>• Talk about things a person might or should do<br>• Listen for, clarify, and respond to job instructions<br>• Talk about job evaluations<br>**Pronunciation:**<br>• Differentiate between helpful and unhelpful responses | **L1:** 0.1.5, 4.1.6, 4.2.1, 4.5.1<br>**L2:** 0.1.5, 4.4.1, 4.5.1<br>**L3:** 0.1.5, 7.5.6,<br>**L4:** 0.1.5, 6.0.3, 6.0.4, 6.1.4, 6.6.6, 7.5.6<br>**L5:** 0.1.2, 0.1.5, 2.5.6, 4.1.6, 4.1.7, 4.3.3, 4.4.1, 4.4.4, 7.4.5, 7.4.7<br>**RE:** 0.1.3, 0.1.5, 4.8.1, 7.2.6, 7.3.3 | **L1:** 35.02, 36.01, 36.05, 36.06, 49.02<br>**L2:** 37.04, 49.01, 49.02, 49.06, 49.16<br>**L3:** 49.01, 49.02<br>**L4:** 35.02, 36.04, 36.05, 49.02, 49.16, 51.05<br>**L5:** 37.01, 37.02, 37.03, 37.04, 40.01, 49.17<br>**RE:** 49.16 | Most SCANS are incorporated into this unit, with an emphasis on:<br>• Knowing how to learn<br>• Seeing things in the mind's eye<br>• Responsibility<br>• Self-management<br>• Interpreting and communicating information | Most EFFs are incorporated into this unit, with an emphasis on:<br>• Using math to solve problems and communicate<br>• Observing critically<br>• Reflecting and evaluating<br>• Solving problems and making decisions<br>• Cooperating with others |
| • Talk about phones and phone calls<br>• Listen for an excuse when calling in sick<br>• Call in sick and give an excuse<br>• Talk about past activities at certain times<br>• Leave and take phone messages<br>• Talk about community services<br>**Pronunciation:**<br>• Differentiate between similar-sounding words | **L1:** 0.1.2, 0.1.5, 1.5.3, 2.1.4, 4.8.1, 7.4.5, 7.5.6<br>**L2:** 0.1.2, 0.1.5, 7.2.5, 7.4.7, 7.5.6<br>**L3:** 0.1.5, 8.2.1, 8.2.3, 8.2.4<br>**L4:** 0.1.2, 0.1.5, 2.1.7, 2.1.8, 6.0.3, 6.0.4, 6.1.4, 7.5.6<br>**L5:** 0.1.2, 0.1.5, 2.1.1, 2.5.6, 7.4.5, 7.5.6, 8.3.2<br>**RE:** 0.1.3, 4.8.1, 7.2.6 | **L1:** 40.05<br>**L2:** 36.02, 49.01, 49.13, 49.16, 49.17<br>**L3:** 49.03, 50.02<br>**L4:** 49.02, 49.16, 51.05<br>**L5:** 40.01, 40.04, 46.01, 49.16<br>**RE:** 49.16, 50.02 | Most SCANS are incorporated into this unit, with an emphasis on:<br>• Seeing things in the mind's eye<br>• Knowing how to learn<br>• Responsibility<br>• Self-management<br>• Interpreting and communicating information | Most EFFs are incorporated into this unit, with an emphasis on:<br>• Observing critically<br>• Using math to solve problems and communicate<br>• Reflecting and evaluating<br>• Solving problems and making decisions |

| Listening & Speaking | CASAS Life Skills Competencies | Standardized Student Syllabi/ LCPs | SCANS Competencies | EFF Content Standards |
|---|---|---|---|---|
| • Talk about containers, weights, and measurements<br>• Listen for prices and quantity of food items<br>• Talk about prices and quantity of food items<br>• Talk about food in your kitchen<br>• Ask for and give the location of supermarket items<br>• Listen for the location of supermarket items<br>• Talk about nutrition and health<br><br>**Pronunciation:**<br>• Syllables in singular and plural nouns | **L1:** 0.1.2, 0.1.5, 1.1.7, 1.3.8, 4.8.1, 7.4.5, 7.5.6<br>**L2:** 0.1.2, 0.1.5, 1.1.6, 1.2.1, 1.2.2, 1.2.5, 1.3.8, 7.2.5, 7.4.7<br>**L3:** 0.1.5, 1.1.1, 1.3.8<br>**L4:** 0.1.5, 1.1.6, 1.3.7, 6.0.3, 6.0.4, 6.1.2, 6.9.2, 7.5.6<br>**L5:** 0.1.2, 0.1.5, 1.2.1, 1.2.2, 1.6.1, 3.5.1, 3.5.2, 7.2.5, 7.4.7<br>**RE:** 0.1.3, 0.1.5, 1.3.8, 4.8.1, 7.2.7, 7.3.3, 7.4.7 | **L1:** 49.01<br>**L2:** 45.01, 45.10, 49.02, 49.06, 49.16, 49.17<br>**L3:** 49.01, 49.13, 50.07<br>**L4:** 45.09, 49.16, 51.05<br>**L5:** 41.06, 45.12, 49.16, 49.17<br>**RE:** 49.16, 49.17, 50.03 | Most SCANS are incorporated into this unit, with an emphasis on:<br>• Seeing things in the mind's eye<br>• Knowing how to learn<br>• Responsibility<br>• Self-management | Most EFFs are incorporated into this unit, with an emphasis on:<br>• Observing critically<br>• Using math to solve problems and communicate<br>• Reflecting and evaluating |
| • Talk about illnesses and symptoms<br>• Listen for appointment dates and times<br>• Make appointments<br>• Talk about causes of accidents<br>• Talk to a pharmacist about prescription information<br>• Listen for prescription information<br>• Talk about accidents and first-aid supplies | **L1:** 0.1.2, 3.1.1, 3.3.1, 4.8.1, 7.4.5<br>**L2:** 0.1.2, 0.1.5, 3.1.1, 3.1.2, 3.5.4, 3.5.5, 7.4.7, 7.5.6<br>**L3:** 0.1.5, 3.1.1<br>**L4:** 0.1.2, 0.1.5, 3.1.1, 3.1.3, 3.3.1, 3.3.2, 3.3.3, 3.4.1, 6.0.2, 6.0.3, 6.0.4, 6.1.3, 7.5.6<br>**L5:** 0.1.2, 0.1.5, 2.5.6, 3.4.3, 4.3.4, 7.4.5, 7.4.7<br>**RE:** 0.1.3, 0.1.5, 4.8.1 | **L1:** 41.03, 49.02<br>**L2:** 41.03, 41.05, 41.08, 49.16, 49.17<br>**L3:** 49.16, 50.02, 50.03<br>**L4:** 41.03, 41.04, 49.02, 49.16<br>**L5:** 40.01, 49.16, 49.17<br>**RE:** 49.16 | Most SCANS are incorporated into this unit, with an emphasis on:<br>• Seeing things in the mind's eye<br>• Knowing how to learn<br>• Responsibility<br>• Self-management | Most EFFs are incorporated into this unit, with an emphasis on:<br>• Observing critically<br>• Using math to solve problems and communicate<br>• Reflecting and evaluating |
| • Talk about ATMs and payment preferences<br>• Talk about home improvement<br>• Talk about reasons for buying things<br>• Return and exchange items in a store<br>• Listen for information to complete a return form<br>• Talk about saving money and organizing bank statements<br><br>**Pronunciation:**<br>• Differentiate between *I like* and *I'd like* | **L1:** 0.1.2, 0.1.5, 1.1.6, 1.3.3, 1.5.3, 1.8.1, 4.8.1, 7.2.4, 7.2.5, 7.4.5, 7.4.7, 7.5.6<br>**L2:** 0.1.2, 0.1.5, 1.2.1, 1.2.2, 1.5.1, 1.5.2, 1.5.3, 7.4.7, 7.5.6, 8.2.6<br>**L3:** 0.1.5, 1.6.3<br>**L4:** 0.1.2, 0.1.5, 1.3.3, 1.6.3, 1.6.4, 6.0.3, 6.0.4, 6.1.2, 7.5.6<br>**L5:** 0.1.5, 0.2.1, 0.2.2, 1.3.2, 1.6.2, 1.8.1, 1.8.2, 7.4.7<br>**RE:** 0.1.3, 0.1.5, 4.8.1, 7.3.3, 7.4.7 | **L1:** 42.04, 42.05, 49.02, 49.16, 49.17<br>**L2:** 44.01, 45.08, 49.16<br>**L3:** 49.16<br>**L4:** 45.06, 49.02, 49.16<br>**L5:** 42.04, 49.16, 49.17<br>**RE:** 49.16, 49.17 | Most SCANS are incorporated into this unit, with an emphasis on:<br>• Seeing things in the mind's eye<br>• Knowing how to learn<br>• Responsibility<br>• Self-management | Most EFFs are incorporated into this unit, with an emphasis on:<br>• Observing critically<br>• Using math to solve problems and communicate<br>• Reflecting and evaluating |

| Unit | Life Skills & Civics Competencies | Vocabulary | Grammar | Critical Thinking & Math Concepts | Reading & Writing |
|---|---|---|---|---|---|
| **Unit 10**<br>**Steps to Citizenship**<br>page 112 | • Identify citizenship requirements<br>• Identify federal, state, and local government officials<br>• Recognize how community participation solves problems<br>• Interpret a flyer<br>• Understand traffic signs<br>• Respond to police and security officers<br>• Understand branches of the U.S. government and term limits | • Citizenship<br>• U.S. government officials<br>• Participants in local government<br>• Types of personal identification<br>• Branches of the U.S. government<br>• Community problems | • *Must* and *must not*<br>• Rules and advice with *must* and *should*<br>• Questions with *have to*<br>• Polite requests with *may, could,* and *can* | • Differentiate between federal, state, and local government officials<br>• Reflect on ways to resolve community problems<br>• Identify dates and times of PTA events<br>• Analyze and calculate term limits for government officials<br><br>**Real-life math:**<br>• Convert spelled-out numbers into numerals<br><br>**Problem solving:**<br>• Determine how to handle traffic violations | • Read about community participation<br>• Write about a community problem<br>• Read a flyer<br>• Write about traffic rules<br>• Write community rules<br>• Read about branches of the U.S. government and term limits<br>• Write about personal IDs and traffic violations |
| **Unit 11**<br>**Deal with Difficulties**<br>page 124 | • Identify crimes and emergencies<br>• Recognize natural disasters<br>• Report and describe emergencies<br>• Fill out accident reports<br>• Make 911 calls<br>• Interpret emergency safety procedures<br>• Identify emergency kit items | • Crimes<br>• Emergencies<br>• Natural disasters<br>• Items on accident reports<br>• 911 emergencies<br>• Items in an emergency kit<br>• Emergency safety procedures | • Review of the simple present, the simple past, and the past continuous<br>• Information questions and *Yes/No* questions with the simple present, the simple past, and the past continuous | • Interpret dates and facts about natural disasters<br>• Differentiate between emergencies and non-emergencies<br>• Draw conclusions about emergency kit items<br>• Choose appropriate action during an emergency<br><br>**Real-life math:**<br>• Interpret a bar chart about home accidents<br><br>**Problem solving:**<br>• Respond appropriately to a hurricane warning | • Read about a fire at home<br>• Write about an emergency<br>• Read about a flood<br>• Read a bar graph about home accidents<br>• Read about emergency safety procedures<br>• Read an emergency kit checklist<br>• Write about a blizzard<br>• Write ideas about emergency procedures |
| **Unit 12**<br>**Take the Day Off**<br>page 136 | • Identify recreational activities<br>• Recognize types of entertainment<br>• Plan weekend activities<br>• Listen and respond to a recorded phone message<br>• Read movie and entertainment brochures<br>• Ask for and give opinions<br>• Interpret admission prices<br>• Identify places to visit in the U.S.<br>• Use a road map | • Recreational activities<br>• Entertainment<br>• Weekend activities<br>• Adjectives expressing opinions | • The superlative<br>• Questions with the superlative<br>• Review of the comparative | • Speculate about weekend activities<br>• Interpret information from an automated phone menu<br>• Negotiate times and dates of recreational activities<br>• Interpret dates and facts about U.S. sights<br>• Calculate distances and travel time<br><br>**Real-life math:**<br>• Calculate admission prices<br><br>**Problem solving:**<br>• Find solutions to reduce time spent watching TV | • Read about weekend activities<br>• Write about weekend plans<br>• Read a brochure<br>• Write opinions about sports<br>• Read a sign with admission prices<br>• Read about places to visit in the U.S.<br>• Read a road map |

| Listening & Speaking | CASAS Life Skills Competencies | Standardized Student Syllabi/ LCPs | SCANS Competencies | EFF Content Standards |
|---|---|---|---|---|
| • Discuss questions about government officials<br>• Listen for information about PTA events<br>• Discuss solutions to community problems<br>• Talk about community rules<br>• Ask and answer questions about ID problems<br>• Listen for information about traffic violations<br>• Talk about government officials | **L1:** 0.1.2, 0.1.5, 2.5.2, 4.8.1, 5.3.6, 5.5.8, 7.2.4, 7.4.5, 7.5.6<br>**L2:** 0.1.5, 5.6.1, 5.6.2, 5.8.1, 7.2.5, 7.4.7, 8.3.2<br>**L3:** 0.1.2, 0.1.5, 1.1.9, 7.4.7, 7.5.6<br>**L4:** 0.1.5, 5.3.7, 5.5.6, 6.0.3, 6.0.4, 6.1.1, 6.1.2<br>**L5:** 0.1.2, 0.1.5, 2.5.6, 4.8.1, 5.5.2, 5.5.3, 5.5.4, 5.5.7, 5.5.8, 7.2.4, 7.4.5<br>**RE:** 0.1.3, 0.1.5, 4.8.1, 7.3.3, 8.3.2 | **L1:** 46.03, 49.01, 49.02<br>**L2:** 46.01, 49.13, 49.16, 49.17, 50.08<br>**L3:** 49.01, 49.16, 49.17<br>**L4:** 49.02, 49.16<br>**L5:** 40.01, 49.01, 49.16<br>**RE:** 49.16 | Most SCANS are incorporated into this unit, with an emphasis on:<br>• Seeing things in the mind's eye<br>• Knowing how to learn<br>• Responsibility<br>• Self-management<br>• Participating as a member of a team | Most EFFs are incorporated into this unit, with an emphasis on:<br>• Observing critically<br>• Using math to solve problems and communicate<br>• Reflecting and evaluating<br>• Solving problems and making decisions |
| • Talk about natural disasters and emergencies<br>• Listen for information about accidents and emergencies<br>• Talk about emergencies<br>• Talk about routines<br>• Listen for information to complete emergency forms<br>• Make 911 calls<br>• Talk about items in emergency kits<br>**Pronunciation:**<br>• Stressed and unstressed syllables | **L1:** 0.1.2, 0.1.5, 2.3.3, 4.8.1, 7.4.5<br>**L2:** 0.1.5, 5.3.8<br>**L3:** 0.1.5<br>**L4:** 0.1.2, 0.1.5, 1.1.3, 2.1.2, 2.5.1, 6.7.2, 7.5.6<br>**L5:** 2.3.3, 2.5.6, 7.4.5, 7.4.7<br>**RE:** 0.1.2, 0.1.3, 0.1.5, 2.3.3, 4.8.1, 7.2.6, 7.3.3 | **L1:** 44.02, 47.01, 49.02, 49.10<br>**L2:** 49.16<br>**L3:** 49.01, 49.03, 50.02<br>**L4:** 40.03, 44.01, 49.02, 49.16<br>**L5:** 40.01, 44.01, 44.02, 49.16, 49.17<br>**RE:** 49.16, 49.17 | Most SCANS are incorporated into this unit, with an emphasis on:<br>• Seeing things in the mind's eye<br>• Knowing how to learn<br>• Responsibility<br>• Self-management | Most EFFs are incorporated into this unit, with an emphasis on:<br>• Observing critically<br>• Using math to solve problems and communicate<br>• Reflecting and evaluating<br>• Solving problems and making decisions |
| • Talk about recreational activities<br>• Listen for information in a recorded phone message<br>• Talk about movies and movie times<br>• Talk about opinions using the superlative<br>• Give opinions about entertainment<br>• Listen for opinions about recreational activities<br>• Talk about distances between places on a map | **L1:** 0.1.5, 2.3.2, 2.6.1, 2.6.3, 4.8.1, 7.4.5<br>**L2:** 0.1.5, 0.2.4, 2.6.1, 7.2.5, 7.4.7<br>**L3:** 0.1.5, 0.2.4, 7.2.4<br>**L4:** 0.1.2, 0.1.5, 2.6.1, 2.6.2, 2.6.3, 6.0.3, 7.5.6<br>**L5:** 0.1.5, 0.2.4, 1.1.3, 1.9.4, 2.5.6, 2.6.3, 5.2.4, 5.2.5, 6.1.3, 6.6.4, 6.6.5, 7.2.5, 7.4.5, 7.4.7<br>**RE:** 0.1.3, 0.1.5, 0.2.4, 2.6.1, 2.6.3, 4.8.1, 7.4.7 | **L1:** 49.02, 49.10<br>**L2:** 49.02, 49.06, 49.13, 49.16, 49.17<br>**L3:** 50.04<br>**L4:** 49.01<br>**L5:** 40.01, 43.03, 49.01, 49.09, 49.16, 49.17<br>**RE:** 49.16, 49.17, 50.04 | Most SCANS are incorporated into this unit, with an emphasis on:<br>• Seeing things in the mind's eye<br>• Knowing how to learn<br>• Responsibility<br>• Self-management | Most EFFs are incorporated into this unit, with an emphasis on:<br>• Observing critically<br>• Using math to solve problems and communicate<br>• Reflecting and evaluating<br>• Solving problems and making decisions |

## A Word or Two About Reading Introductions to Textbooks

*Teaching professionals rarely read a book's introduction.* Instead, we flip through the book's pages, using the pictures, topics, and exercises to determine whether the book matches our learners' needs and our teaching style. We scan the reading passages, conversations, writing tasks, and grammar charts to judge the authenticity and accuracy of the text. At a glance, we assess how easy it would be to manage the pair work, group activities, evaluations, and application tasks.

This Introduction, however, also offers valuable information for the teacher. Because you've read this far, I encourage you to read a little further to learn how *Step Forward's* key concepts, components, and multilevel applications will help you help your learners.

## Step Forward's Key Concepts

### Step Forward is...

- the instructional backbone for single-level and multilevel classrooms.
- a standards-based, performance-based, and topic-based series for low-beginning through high-intermediate learners.
- a source for ready-made, four-skill lesson plans that address the skills our learners need in their workplace, civic, personal, and academic lives.
- a collection of learner-centered, communicative English-language practice activities.

The classroom is a remarkable place. *Step Forward* respects the depth of experience and knowledge that learners bring to the learning process. At the same time, *Step Forward* recognizes that learners' varied proficiencies, goals, interests, and educational backgrounds create instructional challenges for teachers.

To ensure that our learners leave each class having made progress toward their language and life goals, *Step Forward* works from these key concepts:

- **The wide spectrum of learners' needs makes using materials that support multilevel instruction essential.** *Step Forward* works with single-level and multilevel classes.
- **Learners' prior knowledge is a valuable teaching tool.** Prior knowledge questions appear in every *Step Forward* lesson.

- **Learning objectives are the cornerstone of instruction.** Each *Step Forward* lesson focuses on an objective that derives from identified learner needs, correlates to state and federal standards, and connects to a meaningful communication task. Progress toward the objective is evaluated at the end of the lesson.
- **Vocabulary, grammar, and pronunciation skills play an essential role in language learning. They provide learners with the tools needed to achieve life skill, civics, workplace, and academic competencies.** *Step Forward* includes strong vocabulary and grammar strands and features pronunciation and math lesson extensions in each unit.
- **Effective instruction requires a variety of instructional techniques and strategies to engage learners.** Techniques such as Early Production Questioning, Focused Listening, Total Physical Response (TPR), Cooperative Learning, and Problem Solving are embedded in the *Step Forward* series, along with grouping and classroom management strategies.

## The Step Forward Program

The *Step Forward* program has five levels:

- Intro: pre-beginning
- Book 1: low-beginning
- Book 2: high-beginning
- Book 3: low-intermediate
- Book 4: intermediate to high-intermediate

Each level of *Step Forward* correlates to *The Oxford Picture Dictionary*. For pre-literacy learners, *The Basic Oxford Picture Dictionary Literacy Program* provides a flexible, needs-based approach to literacy instruction. Once learners develop strong literacy skills, they will be able to transition seamlessly into *Step Forward Student Introductory Level*.

Each *Step Forward* level includes the following components:

### Step Forward Student Book

A collection of clear, engaging, four-skill lessons based on meaningful learning objectives.

### Step Forward Audio Program

The recorded vocabulary, focused listening, conversations, pronunciation, and reading materials from the *Step Forward Student Book*.

### Step Forward Step-By-Step Lesson Plans with Multilevel Grammar Exercises CD-ROM

An instructional planning resource with interleaved *Step Forward Student Book* pages, detailed lesson plans featuring multilevel teaching strategies and teaching tips, and a CD-ROM of printable multilevel grammar practice for the structures presented in the *Step Forward Student Book*.

### Step Forward Workbook

Practice exercises for independent work in the classroom or as homework.

### Step Forward Multilevel Activity Book

More than 100 photocopiable communicative practice activities and 72 picture cards; lesson materials that work equally well in single-level or multilevel settings.

### Step Forward Test Generator CD-ROM with ExamView® Assessment Suite

Hundreds of multiple choice and life-skill oriented test items for each *Step Forward Student Book*.

## Multilevel Applications of Step Forward

All the *Step Forward* program components support multilevel instruction.

*Step Forward* is so named because it helps learners "step forward" toward their language and life goals, no matter where they start. Our learners often start from very different places and language abilities within the same class.

Regardless of level, all learners need materials that bolster comprehension while providing an appropriate amount of challenge. This makes multilevel materials an instructional necessity in most classrooms.

Each *Step Forward* lesson provides the following multilevel elements:

- **a general topic or competency area** that works across levels. This supports the concept that members of the class community need to feel connected, despite their differing abilities.
- **clear, colorful visuals and realia** that provide pre-level and on-level support during introduction, presentation and practice exercises, as well as prompts for higher-level questions and exercises.

In addition, *Step Forward* correlates to *The Oxford Picture Dictionary* so that teachers can use the visuals and vocabulary from *The Oxford Picture Dictionary* to support and expand upon each lesson.

- **learner-centered practice exercises** that can be used with same-level or mixed-level pairs or small groups. Step Forward exercises are broken down to their simplest steps. Once the exercise has been modeled, learners can usually conduct the exercises themselves.
- **pre-level, on-level, and higher-level objectives for each lesson and the multilevel strategies** necessary to carry out the lesson. These objectives are featured in the *Step-By-Step Lesson Plans*.
- **Grammar Boost pages in the Step Forward Workbook that provide excellent "wait time" activities** for learners who complete an exercise early, thus solving a real issue in the multilevel class.
- **a variety of pair, whole class, and small group activities** in the *Step Forward Multilevel Activity Book*. These activities are perfect for same-level and mixed-level grouping.
- **customizable grammar and evaluation exercises** in *the Step Forward Test Generator CD-ROM with ExamView® Assessment Suite*. These exercises make it possible to create evaluations specific to each level in the class.

## Professional Development

As instructors, we need to reflect on second language acquisition in order to build a repertoire of effective instructional strategies. The *Step Forward Professional Development Program* provides research-based teaching strategies, tasks, and activities for single- and multilevel classes.

## About Writing an ESL Series

It's collaborative! *Step Forward* is the product of dialogs with hundreds of teachers and learners. The dynamic quality of language instruction makes it important to keep this dialog alive. As you use this book in your classes, I invite you to contact me or any member of the *Step Forward* authorial team with your questions or comments.

*Jayme Adelson-Goldstein*

Jayme Adelson-Goldstein, Series Director
Stepforwardteam.us@oup.com

*Step Forward:* **All you need to ensure your learners' success. All the *Step Forward Student Books* follow this format.**

**LESSON 1: VOCABULARY** teaches key words and phrases relevant to the unit topic, and provides conversation practice using the target vocabulary.

New vocabulary is introduced through vibrant art and high-interest listening texts.

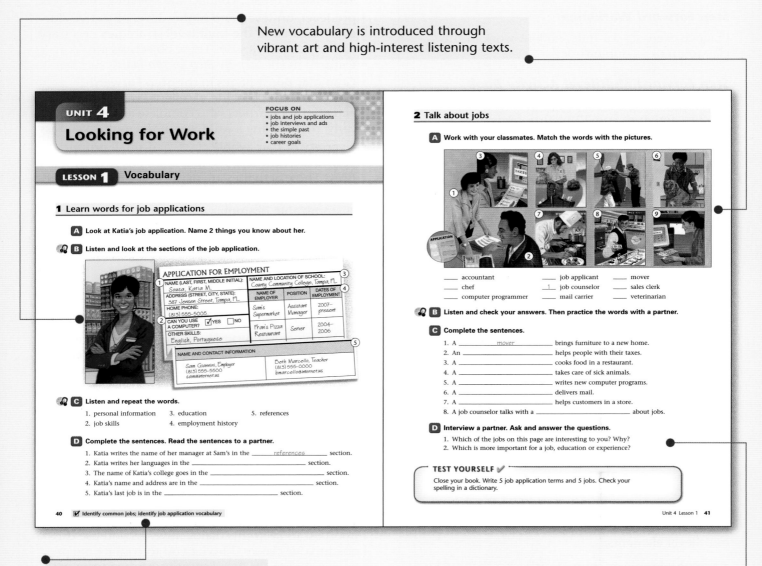

Standards-based objectives are identified at the beginning of every lesson for quick reference.

Learners gain competence in using the new vocabulary through conversation practice.

# LESSON 2: LIFE STORIES expands on vocabulary learned in Lesson 1 and furthers learners' understanding through reading and writing about a life skills topic.

Life skills readings help learners practice the vocabulary in natural contexts.

Learners apply the vocabulary to their own lives by writing about their personal experiences.

---

## LESSON 2 Life stories

### 1 Read about job interviews

**A** Look at the pictures and the title of the story in 1B. What do you think? Will Adam get the job?

**B** Listen and read the story.

**Adam's Job Interviews**

Adam is looking for a job. He goes to job interviews every week. Before the interview, he looks for some information about the company. He also writes some questions: for example, "What will I do?" He always wears nice clothes like a suit or pants with a shirt and tie. He looks clean and neat.

He's sometimes late for interviews, and he usually feels nervous. When he shakes hands, he doesn't make eye contact with the interviewer. He answers all of the questions, but he doesn't smile very much. Adam is confused. He had an interview last week. He felt nervous, but he answered all the questions. He had the right experience and job skills. Why didn't he get the job?

**C** Check your understanding. Adam makes 3 mistakes at job interviews. Check (✔) the mistakes.

- ☐ 1. He writes questions for the job interview.
- ☐ 2. He wears nice clothes.
- ☑ 3. He's sometimes late for interviews.
- ☐ 4. He doesn't look at the interviewer.
- ☐ 5. He answers all of the questions.
- ☐ 6. He doesn't smile very much.

---

### 2 Write about a job interview

**A** Think about a job interview. Answer the questions. Write your answers in a paragraph.

¹ What do you do before a job interview? ² What do you wear to the interview? ³ Do you arrive late or on time? ⁴ How do you feel? ⁵ Do you like to go to job interviews?

Before a job interview, I _____

_____

_____

**Need help?**

I feel...
cheerful.
worried.
confident.
happy.
nervous.

**B** Read your paragraph to a partner. Does your partner like interviews?

### 3 Interpret a job ad

**A** Listen. Check (✔) the correct information about each job.

| Job | Part-time | Full-time | References required |
|-----|-----------|-----------|---------------------|
| Chef | | | |
| Sales clerk | | | |

**B** Read the job ad. Complete the sentences. Use the words in the box.

| part-time | experience | immediately | references |
|---|---|---|---|

**WANTED:**
Assistant breakfast chef, p/t 6 a.m.–10 a.m., exp. and written refs required, start immed.

1. The hours are from 6 a.m. to 10 a.m. It's a _____ job.
2. You need written _____ for this job.
3. _____ is also required.
4. They need someone right now. The job starts _____ .

**C** Listen. Then practice the conversation with a partner. Use your own ideas.

A: I want to work at the front desk in a hotel.
B: What skills do you need for that job?
A: I need to speak English and know how to use a computer.

**Need help?**

I want...
to work at the front desk in a hotel.
to be an accountant.

**TEST YOURSELF** ✔

Close your book. Write 2 things you should do and 2 things you shouldn't do before and during an interview. Tell a partner.

*Test Yourself*, at the end of every lesson, provides learners with ongoing self-assessment.

# LESSON 3: GRAMMAR provides clear, simple presentation of the target structure followed by thorough, meaningful practice of it.

Clear grammar charts and exercises help learners develop language confidence and accuracy.

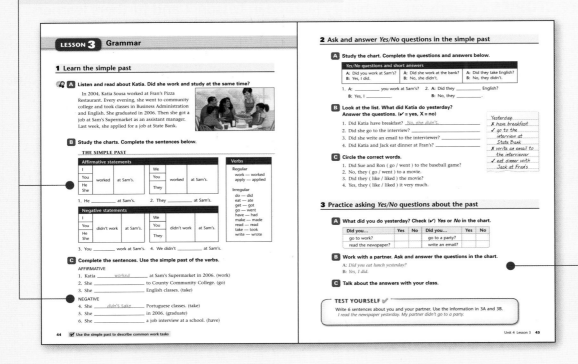

Learners work together to increase fluency and accuracy, using the grammar point to talk about themselves.

# LESSON 4: EVERYDAY CONVERSATION provides learners with fluent, authentic conversations to increase familiarity with natural English.

Pronunciation activities focus on common areas of difficulty.

Model dialogs feature authentic examples of everyday conversation.

Listening activities build listening skills.

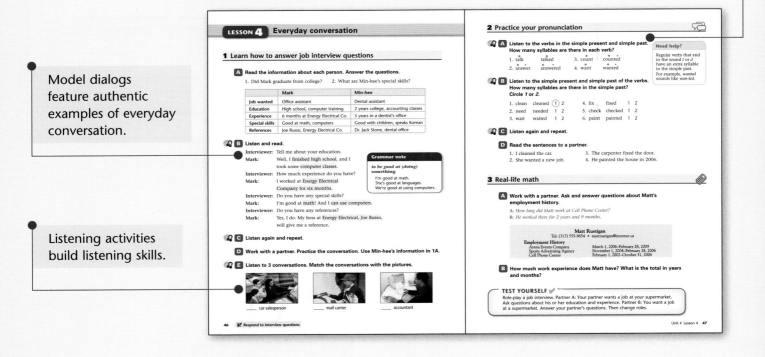

## LESSON 5: REAL-LIFE READING develops essential reading skills and offers both life skill and pre-academic reading materials.

High-interest readings recycle vocabulary and grammar.

Chart literacy is increased through practice reading and understanding different types of charts.

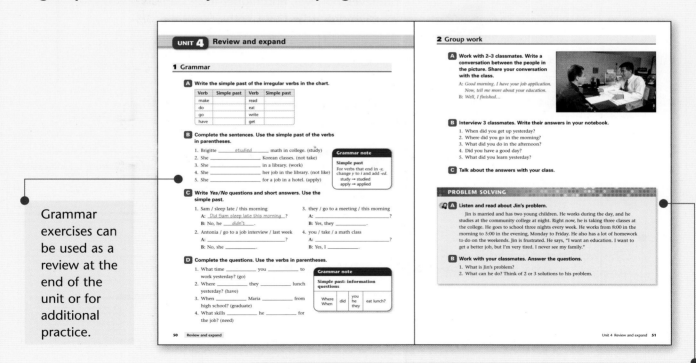

## REVIEW AND EXPAND includes additional grammar practice and communicative group tasks to ensure your learners' progress.

Grammar exercises can be used as a review at the end of the unit or for additional practice.

Problem solving tasks encourage learners to use critical thinking skills and meaningful discussion to find solutions to common problems.

# Step Forward offers many different components.

## Step-By-Step Lesson Plans

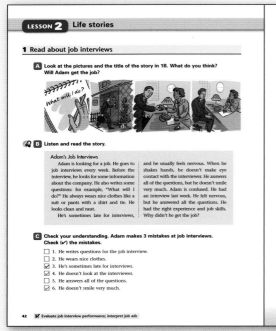

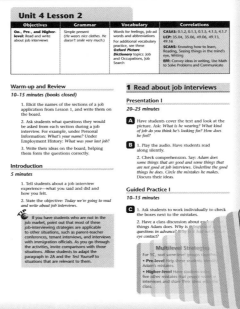

The *Step-By-Step Lesson Plans* provide tips and strategies for conducting *Student Book* activities and applying the lesson to the multilevel classroom.

**Multilevel Strategies**

For 1C, seat same-level groups together.
- **Pre-level** Help these students identify Adam's mistakes.
- **Higher-level** Have students write five other mistakes that people make at interviews and share their ideas with the class.

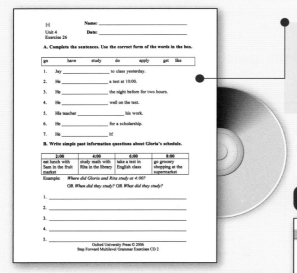

The *Multilevel Grammar Exercises CD-ROM*, a free CD-ROM included with the *Step-By-Step Lesson Plans*, offers additional exercises for pre-level, on-level, and higher-level learners for each grammar point in the *Student Book*.

## Workbook

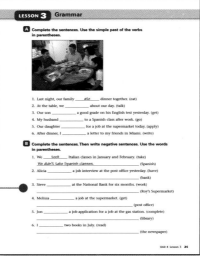

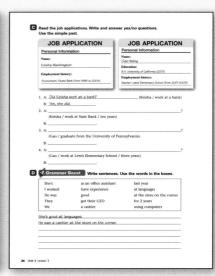

The *Workbook* offers additional exercises ideal for independent practice, homework, or review.

## Multilevel Activity Book

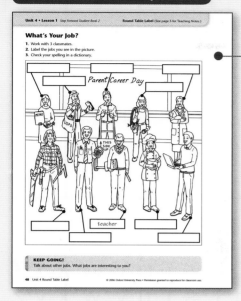

The *Multilevel Activity Book* features over 100 reproducible communication activities to complement the multilevel classroom through a variety of pair, small group, and whole-class activities.

There are over 140 picture cards in the *Multilevel Activity Book* that are perfect for practicing key vocabulary and grammar.

## Audio Program

Audio CDs and Cassettes feature the listening exercises from the *Student Book* as well as conversations, pronunciation, and readings.

## Test Generator

The *Test Generator CD-ROM with ExamView® Assessment Suite* offers hundreds of test items for each *Student Book*. Teachers can print out ready-made tests or create their own tests.

## Professional Development

### Professional Development Task 8

Imagine you want your learners to practice listening carefully during a group task. One behavior you could demonstrate would be leaning forward. Make a list of at least three other behaviors or expressions that careful listeners use.

The *Professional Development Program* offers instructors research-based teaching strategies and activities for single- and multilevel classes, plus Professional Development Tasks like this one.

# The First Step

**FOCUS ON**

- the alphabet
- greeting and saying goodbye
- the verb *be*
- personal information
- days and months

## Let's get started

## 1 Review the alphabet

**A** **Listen. Repeat the letters of the alphabet.**

A B C D E F G H I J K L M N O P Q R S T U V W X Y Z
a b c d e f g h i j k l m n o p q r s t u v w x y z

**B** **Work with a partner. Choose a word in the box.**
**Ask: *How do you spell...?***

| chair | table | desk | pencil | board | homework |
|-------|-------|------|--------|-------|----------|

**A:** *How do you spell chair?*
**B:** *C-H-A-I-R.*

## 2 Meet, greet, and say goodbye

**A** **Listen and read.**

Denise: Hello, Rick! How are you?
Rick: Fine, thank you!
Elena: Good morning!
Denise: Oh hi, Elena! Elena, this is Rick.
Rick: Hello, Elena. It's nice to meet you.
Elena: Nice to meet you, too.
Rick: Well, we're late for class. We have to go.
Goodbye.
Elena: See you later!

**B** **Work in groups of 3. Practice the conversation. Use your own names.**

☑ Respond to personal information questions; identify days and months

## 3 The verb *be*

**Complete the sentences with *am, is,* or *are*. Use contractions when possible.**

1. I 'm_____ fine.
2. You _____ happy.
3. We _____ in class.

4. Elena and Sam _____ married.
5. I _____ at school.
6. Elena _____ a new student.

## 4 Personal information

**Look at the student ID card. Work with a partner. Ask and answer the questions.**

1. What's her first name? _Vera_____
2. What's her last name? _____
3. What's her address? _____
4. What's her phone number? _____
5. Where does she go to school? _____

Eastside Adult School

First name: **Vera**
Last name: **Wong**
Address:
1530 Hill St.
Los Angeles, CA 90001
Phone:
213-555-4768

## 5 Days and months

STUDENT AUDIO

**A** **Write the missing days and months. Then listen and check.**

Days of the week:
Sunday ___Monday___ Tuesday _____ Thursday _____ Saturday

Months of the year:
January ___February___ March _____ May _____
July _____ September _____ November _____

**B** **Work with a partner. Follow the directions. Use the days and months in 5A.**

1. Circle the day and month today.
2. Check (✔) the months with 30 days.

STUDENT AUDIO

**C** **Listen and read.**

A: When is your birthday?
B: It's November 1st.
A: What day is that this year?
B: Thursday.

**D** **Work with a partner. Practice the conversation. Use your own information.**

| Ordinal numbers | |
|---|---|
| 1–first | 11–eleventh |
| 2–second | 12–twelfth |
| 3–third | 13–thirteenth |
| 4–fourth | 14–fourteenth |
| 5–fifth | 15–fifteenth |
| 6–sixth | 16–sixteenth |
| 7–seventh | 17–seventeenth |
| 8–eighth | 18–eighteenth |
| 9–ninth | 19–nineteenth |
| 10–tenth | 20–twentieth |

UNIT **1**

# Learning to Learn

**FOCUS ON**
- ways to learn new words
- learning styles
- the simple present
- introductions
- setting goals

**LESSON 1** **Vocabulary**

## 1 Learn ways to learn new words

**A** Look at the pictures. Name the classroom objects you see.

STUDENT AUDIO

**B** Listen and look at the pictures.

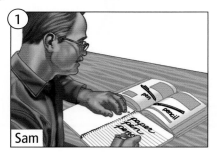
1 Sam

2 Dana
pen

3 Linda
pen  book
Write  Read

4 Naomi
Learn English

5 Fernando
chalk?
chalk

6 Ahmed

STUDENT AUDIO

**C** Listen and repeat the words.

1. copy new words
2. practice with a partner
3. brainstorm words
4. use a computer
5. look up words
6. listen to CDs

**D** Complete the sentences. Read the sentences to a partner.

1. Naomi likes to _____use a computer_____.
2. Fernando likes to _____ in the dictionary.
3. Dana likes to _____.
4. Linda and her friends like to _____.
5. Ahmed likes to _____.
6. Sam likes to _____.

4    ☑ Identify personal learning styles

## 2 Talk about learning tools

**A** Work with your classmates. Match the words with the picture.

_____ CD player    _1_ flashcards    _____ notebook

_____ chart    _____ group    _____ pair

_____ dictionary    _____ the Internet    _____ picture

STUDENT AUDIO

**B** Listen and check your answers. Then practice the words with a partner.

**C** Look at the picture. Mark the sentences **T** (true) or **F** (false).

_T_ 1. One student is using flashcards with her partner.

_____ 2. A group is listening to CDs on the CD player.

_____ 3. One student is looking up _chalk_ in the dictionary.

_____ 4. One student is making a chart.

_____ 5. Five students are writing in their notebooks.

_____ 6. One pair of students is working on the Internet.

**D** Work with a partner. Practice the conversation. Use your own information.

A: How do you learn new words?

B: I use flashcards. How about you?

A: I listen to CDs.

**Need help?**

I...
use a computer.
go on the Internet.
make a chart.

**TEST YOURSELF** ✔

Close your book. Write 4 ways to learn new words and 6 learning tools. Check your spelling in a dictionary.

## 1 Read about learning a language

**A** Look at the pictures and the title of the story in 1B. Guess the answers to the questions.

1. What is Dan doing?
2. How does Dan like to learn?

 **B** Listen and read the story.

### Learning a New Language
### by Dan Tanaka

I practice English every day. In the morning, I listen to conversations on my CD player. I listen and repeat the new words, but sometimes I forget the words I learn.

I also like to read. In my English class, we read a lot of stories. I always underline the new words. Then I copy the new words in my notebook.

I'm a good listener, but I don't speak a lot. It is easy to read English, but I want to speak more. I'm going to ask more questions in class.

**C** Check your understanding. Mark the sentences T (true) or F (false).

___F___ 1. Dan is learning to speak Japanese.

_____ 2. He practices English every day.

_____ 3. He never forgets new words.

_____ 4. He likes to read.

_____ 5. He isn't a good listener.

_____ 6. He speaks a lot.

☑ Identify effective study strategies

## 2 Write about learning English

**A** **Think about how you learn English. Answer the questions. Write your answers in a paragraph. Give the paragraph a title.**

[1] How often do you practice English?  [2] What do you listen to?  [3] What do you read?  [4] Do you practice alone or with other people?  [5] What is easy and what is difficult for you in English?

How I Practice English

I practice English every day. I listen to English on the radio. I read stories in English. I usually practice with

_____

I practice _____

_____

_____

_____

_____

**B** **Read your paragraph to a partner. What is easy for your partner?**

## 3 Talk about learning styles

**A** **Listen to Dan and Min talk about how they learn. Check (✔) the answers.**

| Who likes to... | Dan | Min | Who likes to... | Dan | Min |
|---|---|---|---|---|---|
| draw pictures of new words? | | ✔ | say new words? | | |
| see new words? | | | write new words? | | |
| hear new words? | | | put new words in a chart? | | |

**B** **How do you like to learn English? Check (✔) the things that you do.**

☐ 1. I go on the Internet.  ☐ 4. I talk with classmates.
☐ 2. I watch movies.  ☐ 5. I make charts.
☐ 3. I read stories.  ☐ 6. I listen to CDs or cassettes.

**C** **Listen. Then practice the conversation with a partner. Use your own ideas.**

A: How do you like to learn?
B: I like to watch movies. How about you?
A: I like to listen to CDs or cassettes.

**TEST YOURSELF** ✓

Close your book. Write 3 ways you like to learn and 3 ways you don't like to learn. Tell a partner.

# 1 Learn the simple present with *want to, like to, need to*

**A** Listen and read the conversation. Answer the questions.

1. Does Cam Tu want to study grammar or listen to music?
2. Does Brenda need to study the simple present or the simple past?

**Cam Tu:** Hi, Brenda. I'm looking for a study partner. Do you want to work together after class?

**Brenda:** Yes, I do. I really don't like to study grammar, but I need to study the simple present.

**Cam Tu:** No problem. I need to study grammar, too.

**Brenda:** Okay. We can use my book.

**B** Study the charts. Circle the correct words in the sentences below.

### THE SIMPLE PRESENT WITH *WANT TO, LIKE TO, NEED TO*

| Affirmative statements | | | | | |
|---|---|---|---|---|---|
| I<br>You<br>We<br>They | want<br>like<br>need | to study. | He<br>She | wants<br>likes<br>needs | to study. |

1. You need ( study /(to study)).  2. She ( wants / want ) to study.

| Negative statements | | | | | | |
|---|---|---|---|---|---|---|
| I<br>You<br>We<br>They | don't | want<br>like<br>need | to study. | He<br>She | doesn't | want<br>like<br>need | to study. |

3. They don't ( like / like to ) study.  4. He ( don't / doesn't ) want to study.

**C** Complete the sentences. Use the words in parentheses.

1. Brenda _____*needs to study*_____ the simple present. (need, study)
2. Cam Tu _____ alone. (not want, work)
3. Cam Tu and Brenda _____ together. (want, work)
4. Cam Tu _____ grammar. (like, study)
5. Brenda and Cam Tu _____ two books. (not need, use)

☑ Use the simple present to describe study habits

## 2 Ask and answer information questions

**A** Study the charts. Complete the questions and answers below.

| Information questions and answers | |
|---|---|
| **A:** What do you like to study? **B:** I like to study vocabulary. | **A:** When do you like to study? **B:** We like to study in the evening. |
| **A:** Where does she like to study? **B:** She likes to study in the kitchen. | **A:** How do they like to study? **B:** They like to study with flashcards. |

1. **A:** ___How does___ Brenda like to study?

   **B:** She ___likes to study___ with a partner.

2. **A:** _____ Brenda like to study?

   **B:** She _____ grammar.

3. **A:** _____ you like to study?

   **B:** I _____ in the kitchen.

4. **A:** _____ they like to study?

   **B:** They _____ in the evening.

**B** Match the questions with the answers.

__c__ 1. What does she need to study?

_____ 2. When do they want to meet?

_____ 3. How does he like to learn?

_____ 4. Where do they want to meet?

_____ 5. What do they want to learn?

a. They want to meet at school.

b. They want to learn grammar.

c. She needs to study ten new words.

d. He likes to use flashcards.

e. They want to meet in the morning.

## 3 Practice asking information questions

**A** Read the questions. Write your answers in your notebook.

1. What do you need to study?
2. Where do you like to study?
3. What do you want to study?
4. How do you like to study?

*1. I need to study vocabulary.*

**B** Interview a partner. Ask and answer the questions in 3A.

**A:** *What do you need to study?*
**B:** *I need to study vocabulary.*

**C** Talk about the answers with your class.

**TEST YOURSELF** ✔

Ask a partner: How do you like to study? What languages do you want to learn? What learning tools do you need to use?

## 1 Learn how to check what you hear

 **A** **Listen to the conversations. Write the correct names in the blanks.**

Kenji

Haruko

Mr. Singh

_____

Ms. Morgan

Chanda

Barbara

_____

**B** **Listen again. Match the people with the questions.**

_____ 1. Haruko      a. What's your name again?

_____ 2. Ms. Morgan   b. Excuse me? What's your name?

_____ 3. Barbara     c. How do you spell your first name?

 **C** **Listen and read.**

**Ned:**    Hi, everyone. I want to introduce my friend Emmy.

**Rita:**    What's your name again?

**Emmy:**  Emmy.

**Rita:**    E-M-M-Y?

**Emmy:**  That's right.

**Rita:**    Hi, Emmy. I'm Rita, and this is Alma.

**Emmy:**  Nice to meet you.

**D** **Listen again and repeat.**

**E** **Work with a partner. Practice the conversation. Introduce your partner to 2 classmates.**

## 2 Practice your pronunciation

 **A** **Listen to the falling and rising intonation. Then listen again and repeat.**

1. What's your name? ↘

2. My name's Emmy. E-M-M-Y. ↘

3. What's your name again? ↗

4. Emmy? E-M-M-Y? ↗

 **B** **Read the conversation. Check (✔) *Falling* or *Rising*. Then listen and check your answers.**

| | Falling ↘ | Rising ↗ |
|---|---|---|
| **A:** Hi, I'm Kenji . | ✔ | |
| **B:** What's your name again? | | ✔ |
| **A:** Kenji . | | |
| **B:** K-E-N-J-I ? | | |
| **A:** Yes. What's your name? | | |
| **B:** Anga. | | |
| **A:** Excuse me? | | |
| **B:** Anga. A-N-G-A. | | |
| **A:** Oh. Nice to meet you, Anga. | | |

**Need help?**

**Falling and rising intonation**

Statements and information questions usually use falling intonation.

Use rising intonation to check your understanding.

**C** **Work with a partner. Practice the conversation with your own names. Use falling and rising intonation.**

## 3 Real-life math

**A** **Read and answer the questions.**

1. Anga wants to learn the names of her 35 classmates. She has five days. How many names does she need to learn every day?

    35 names ÷ 5 days = _____ names per day

2. Achir likes to learn new words. He learns three new words every day. How many words does he learn in one week?

    3 words x 7 days = _____ words per week

**B** **Read your answers to a partner.**

*35 names divided by 5 days equals…*

**TEST YOURSELF** ✓

Role-play introductions. Meet the students in your class. Partner A: Introduce your partner to 5 classmates. Partner B: Greet your classmates. Then change roles. Meet more classmates.

## 1 Get ready to read

**A** Read the definitions.

goal: something you want to do, be, or learn
plan: an idea or list of how to do something

recipe: instructions for cooking something
set a goal: make a goal; decide on a goal

**B** Look at the pictures. Match the people's goals with the pictures.

_c_ 1. Cesar: talk to his co-workers     ____ 3. Fatima: read to her children

____ 2. Jay: read a recipe     ____ 4. Donaldo: use the Internet

## 2 Read about goals

**A** Read the article.

# Setting Goals

Goals help us do the things we want to do. Long-term goals are the big goals—a new job or a house. Short-term goals are the small goals—learn ten new words or save $10 every week.

Steve wants to be a chef.[1] That is his long-term goal. For this goal, he needs to read cookbooks in English. Steve's first short-term goal is: Read a recipe and prepare the food. Steve's plan for his short-term goal has three steps.[2]

Steve plans to try more recipes and take cooking classes. Then he can get a job as a chef. Steve sets short-term goals. They are the steps to his long-term goal.

[1] chef: a cook in a restaurant
[2] step: a part of a plan

**SHORT-TERM GOAL: READ A RECIPE AND PREPARE THE FOOD**

| STEPS | COMPLETE BY |
|---|---|
| 1. Read a recipe and look up new words in the dictionary. | March 13th |
| 2. Ask my teacher for help with new words. | March 15th |
| 3. Use the recipe to cook the food for my family. | March 17th |

STUDENT AUDIO

**B** Listen and read the article again.

**C** **Mark the sentences T (true) or F (false).**

___T___ 1. "Learn ten new words" is an example of a short-term goal.

_____ 2. There are two steps in Steve's plan.

_____ 3. Steve's long-term goal is to look up words in the dictionary.

_____ 4. Steve wants to read a recipe.

**D** **Complete the sentences. Use the words in the box.**

| set   steps   ~~goals~~   plan |

1. _Goals_ can help you learn or do something.

2. We _____ short-term goals and long-term goals.

3. It's important to make a _____ for your goals.

4. A plan can have many _____.

## 3 Set a goal and make a plan

**A** **Read the short-term goals in the chart. Add 2 more short-term goals to the chart.**

| Goals | |
|---|---|
| 1. Open a bank account. | 5. Ask for directions on the street. |
| 2. Order food in a restaurant. | 6. Understand a TV program in English. |
| 3. Listen to a song and write the words. | 7. My goal: _____ |
| 4. Talk to a doctor or dentist. | 8. My goal: _____ |

**B** **Choose a goal. Make a plan. Then complete the chart.**

| My goal: _____ | |
|---|---|
| Steps | Complete by |
| 1. | |
| 2. | |
| 3. | |

**C** **Talk about your goals and your plans with the class.**

*My goal is: Learn to use a computer. My plan has three steps.*

**BRING IT TO LIFE**

Talk to 2 friends or family members about their goals. Tell your classmates about the goals.

## 1 Grammar

**A** Complete the questions and answers. Use the words in parentheses.

1. A: <u>Do</u> you <u>like to study</u>
   in groups? (like to study)

   B: Yes, <u>I do</u>.

2. A: _____ she _____
   new words? (like to look up)

   B: No, _____.

3. A: _____ they _____
   pronunciation? (want to practice)

   B: Yes, _____.

4. A: _____ he _____
   grammar? (need to study)

   B: Yes, _____.

> **Grammar note**
>
> *Yes/No questions and answers*
> A: Do you like to read books?
> B: Yes, I do. *or* No, I don't.
>
> A: Does he like to write?
> B: Yes, he does. *or* No, he doesn't.

**B** Circle the correct words.

1. ( (They) / He ) always look up new words in the dictionary.
2. ( You / She ) practices English every day.
3. ( I / He ) likes to read stories.
4. ( She / We ) listen to CDs in the evening.

**C** Look at the answers. Complete the questions with *what, when, where,* or *how*.

1. A: <u>How</u> do you like to study?
   B: With a partner.

2. A: _____ do you like to study?
   B: In the morning.

3. A: _____ do you like to study?
   B: In the library.

4. A: _____ do you like to study?
   B: Grammar.

**D** Complete the sentences with *in, on,* or *to*.

1. We like to go _____<u>on</u>_____ the Internet.
2. She likes to listen _____ CDs.
3. They like to work _____ pairs.
4. I like to write words _____ my notebook.

## 2 Group work

**A** Work with 2–3 classmates. Write 2 short conversations between the people in the picture. Share your conversations with the class.

A: *Hi, Ratana. I want to introduce my friend Rick.*

B: *Hi, Rick. I'm...*

**B** What are some good ideas for learning English? Interview 4 classmates. Write their ideas in your notebook.

A: *Hi, Alexa. What is one idea for learning English?*

B: *I like to listen to the news every day.*

A: *That's a good idea.*

*Alexa—listen to the news*

**C** Talk about the ideas with your class.

*Alexa likes to listen to the news.*

---

### PROBLEM SOLVING

**A** Listen and read about Noreen's problem.

Noreen works full-time every day. She also has a part-time job on the weekend. She goes to school three nights a week. She likes her class and her teacher. But Noreen is usually very tired after work. She can't do her homework, and then she can't get good grades.

**B** Work with your classmates. Answer the questions.

1. What is Noreen's problem?
2. What can she do? Think of 2 or 3 solutions to her problem.

# Getting Together

**FOCUS ON**
- feelings and weather
- schedules and events
- the future with *will*
- asking for directions
- small talk and invitations

## LESSON 1 Vocabulary

## 1 Learn words for feelings

**A** Look at the pictures. Where are the people?

**B** Listen and look at the pictures.

1. Dan

2. Jim

3. Tara

4. Gloria

5. Rob

6. Priya

**C** Listen and repeat the words.

1. bored    2. frustrated    3. sleepy    4. surprised    5. cheerful    6. upset

**D** Complete the sentences. Read the sentences to a partner.

1. It's a sunny day. Rob is _____cheerful_____.
2. Fernando gives Gloria some flowers. She's _____.
3. Jim is late for work. He's _____.
4. There's a tree on Priya's car! She's _____.
5. It's raining. Dan can't go out. He's _____.
6. It's dark and cloudy out. Tara's _____.

## 2 Talk about the weather

**A** **Work with your classmates. Match the words with the pictures.**

80°F/27°C  (1)  (2)
(3)  (4) 32°F/0°C
(6) 50°F/10°C
(8) 102°F/39°C Humidity 98% (9)
(7)
(5)

____ cool          ____ hot          ____ lightning
____ foggy         ____ humid        ____ snowstorm
____ freezing      ____ icy          __1__ thunderstorm

**B** **Listen and check your answers. Then practice the words with a partner.**

**C** **Look at the pictures in 2A. Complete the conversations.**

1. **A:** Wow! It's raining a lot. This is a bad _thunderstorm_!
   **B:** Yes, and look at the _____. Let's go into the house!

2. **A:** Brrr. It's 32 degrees. It's _____. Be careful. The sidewalk is _____.
   **B:** OK. I love a good _____. The city looks so white and clean.

3. **A:** I'm so frustrated. I can't see anything. It's very _____.
   **B:** And I need a sweater. It's _____ outside.

4. **A:** Ugh! It's 102 degrees. It's so _____!
   **B:** I know. And with 98% humidity. I hate _____ weather.

**D** **Interview a partner. Ask and answer the questions.**

1. How do you usually feel on hot, humid days?
2. How do you usually feel on cool, foggy days?

---

**TEST YOURSELF** ✔

Close your book. Write 5 words for feelings and 5 words for the weather.
Check your spelling in a dictionary.

## 1 Read about a favorite season

**A** **Look at the pictures and the title of the story in 1B. Circle *a* or *b*.**

1. Ana's favorite season is probably _____.
   a. winter
   b. summer

2. The story talks about _____.
   a. a baseball game
   b. a music festival

 **B** **Listen and read the story.**

My Favorite Season
by Ana Diaz

Summer is my favorite season. In summer, the weather is warm and sunny. I usually feel cheerful on sunny days. There are many things to do in the summer, too. In July, my friends and I often go to the International Music Festival in the park. Musicians come from all over the world. This year the festival will be on Saturday and Sunday, July 30th and 31st. My favorite band, the Jumping Jacks, will play in the afternoon. We'll probably have a picnic in the park before the concert.

The County Fair is in August. I take my vacation in August after the fair. Imagine that! No work for one week! This year I want to visit my friends in Mexico.

**C** **Check your understanding. Mark the sentences T (true) or F (false).**

_F_ 1. In summer, Ana often feels bored.

_____ 2. The International Music Festival is in the park.

_____ 3. Ana's favorite band is the Jumping Jacks.

_____ 4. The County Fair is in August.

_____ 5. Ana takes her vacation before the County Fair.

> **Grammar note**
>
> **Prepositions of time**
> *before*
>    Sunday is before Monday.
>
> *after*
>    Tuesday is after Monday.

## 2 Write about events in your favorite season

**A** Think about your favorite season. Complete the paragraph.

<u>My Favorite Season</u>

_____ is my favorite season.
In _____, the weather
is _____. There are many things to do.
I can _____. I like
to _____, too.

**Need help?**

**Seasons of the year**
My favorite season is...

spring.          fall.

summer.          winter.

**B** Read your paragraph to a partner. What is your partner's favorite season?

## 3 Use a calendar

**A** Listen. Write these events and times on the calendar.

| fair | baseball game | ~~music festival~~ | 9:00 a.m. | ~~11:00 a.m.~~ | 8:00 p.m. |

### JULY

| Mon. 25 | Tues. 26 | Wed. 27 | Thurs. 28 | Fri. 29 | Sat. 30 | Sun. 31 |
|---------|----------|---------|-----------|---------|---------|---------|
|         |          |         |           |         |         | music festival 11:00 a.m. |

### AUGUST

| Mon. 1 | Tues. 2 | Wed. 3 | Thurs. 4 | Fri. 5 | Sat. 6 | Sun. 7 |
|--------|---------|--------|----------|--------|--------|--------|
|        |         |        |          |        |        |        |

**B** Listen. Then practice the conversation with a partner. Use the information in the calendar.

**A:** Do you want to go to the music festival?

**B:** Sure. When is it?

**A:** It's on July 30th and 31st.

**TEST YOURSELF** ✔

Close your book. Write the dates and times for 3 things you will do next week. Tell a partner.

Unit 2 Lesson 2   **19**

## 1 Learn the future with *will*

**A** Listen and read. When will the Jumping Jacks be at River Stadium?

In July, the Jumping Jacks will play at the Riverside Restaurant and in Bridge Street Park. In August, their first concerts will be at River Stadium on the 5th and 6th. They won't play at River Stadium on August 7th. That day they'll be at the County Fair. The concert at the County Fair will start at 5:00 and will end at 8:00.

**JUMPING JACKS**
SCHEDULE

**July 8–9**
Riverside Restaurant
8:00 p.m.

**July 30–31**
Bridge Street Park
3:00 p.m.

**August 5–6**
River Stadium
9:00 p.m.

**August 7**
County Fair
5:00-8:00 p.m.

**B** Study the charts. Complete the sentences below.

### THE FUTURE WITH *WILL*

| Affirmative statements | | | | | | | Contractions |
|---|---|---|---|---|---|---|---|
| I You He She It | will | start at 8:00. | | We You They | will | start at 8:00. | will = 'll<br>I'll start at 8:00.<br>They'll start at 8:00. |

1. She _____will_____ start at 8:00.   2. They will _____ at 8:00.

| Negative statements | | | | | | | Contractions |
|---|---|---|---|---|---|---|---|
| I You He She It | will not | start at 6:00. | | We You They | will not | start at 6:00. | will not = won't<br>You won't start at 6:00.<br>He won't start at 6:00. |

3. He _____ at 6:00.   4. We won't _____ at 6:00.

**C** Complete the sentences with *will ('ll)* or *won't* and the verbs in parentheses. Use the Jumping Jacks schedule in 1A.

1. The concert at the Riverside Restaurant _____won't start_____ at 6:00 p.m. (start)

2. The Jumping Jacks _____ in Bridge Street Park on July 30th. (be)

3. The Jumping Jacks _____ at River Stadium in July. (play)

4. We _____ the Jumping Jacks at River Stadium on August 5th. (see)

✔ Use the future with *will* and *won't* to describe future plans

## 2 Ask and answer questions with *will*

**A** Study the charts. Listen and repeat the conversations.

| Information questions and answers |
| --- |
| **A:** When will they play? <br> **B:** They'll play at 7:00. |
| **A:** What time will the concert start? <br> **B:** It'll start at 5:00. |

| *Yes/No* questions and short answers |
| --- |
| **A:** Will they play in the park? <br> **B:** No, they won't. |
| **A:** Will the concert end at 8:00? <br> **B:** Yes, it will. |

**B** Read Peter's "Yearly Planner." Complete the questions and answers.

INFORMATION QUESTIONS AND ANSWERS

1. **A:** When _____will_____ Peter _____start_____ school?

   **B:** _He'll start school in September._

2. **A:** When _____ Peter _____ his brother?

   **B:** _____

*YES/NO* QUESTIONS AND SHORT ANSWERS

3. **A:** _Will_____ Peter's sisters _____ him in December?

   **B:** _____

4. **A:** _____ Peter _____ on vacation in December?

   **B:** _____

**Yearly Planner**

SEPTEMBER
*start school*

OCTOBER
*visit my brother*

NOVEMBER
*my sisters visit*

DECEMBER
*go on vacation*

## 3 Practice questions with *will*

**A** Read the questions. Write your answers in your notebook.

1. Where will you be at this time tomorrow?
2. Where will you be at this time next week?
3. Where will you be five years from now?

**Need help?**

**Time expressions**
Now it's Monday at 8 p.m.
   this time tomorrow = Tuesday at 8 p.m.

Now it's 2007.
   five years from now = 2012

**B** Interview a partner. Ask and answer the questions in 3A.

**A:** *Where will you be at this time tomorrow?*
**B:** *I'll be at home.*

**TEST YOURSELF** ✔

Write 6 sentences about you and about your partner. Use the ideas in 3A and 3B.
*At this time tomorrow, I'll be at home. Samuel will be at school.*

## 1 Learn how to give and get directions

**A** Look at the pictures. Match the directions with the pictures.

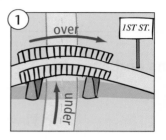
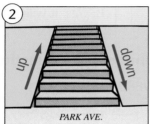
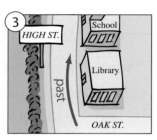
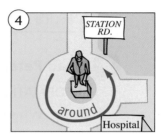

_____ Go past the library.        _____ Go around the traffic circle.

_____ Go up the steps.        __1__ Go over the bridge.

**B** Look at the map. Then listen and read.

**A:** Excuse me. How do I get to the bank from here?

**B:** Go straight on 1st Street. Then go over the bridge and turn right.

**A:** Go over the bridge and turn right?

**B:** Yes, that's it. Then go past the pharmacy. The bank is on the right.

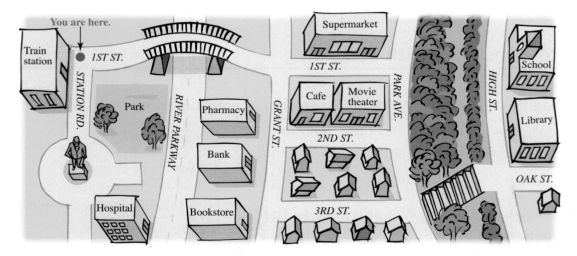

**C** Listen again and repeat.

**D** Work with a partner. Practice the conversation. Give directions from the train station to the school and the hospital.

**E** Listen to the conversation between Sara and Jenny. Find the route on the map in 1B. Where is Sara's house? What color is it?

## 2 Practice your pronunciation

 **A** Listen to the stressed words in these conversations.

1. **A:** Do I take the next street on the left?
   **B:** No, take the <u>second</u> street on the left.

2. **A:** Do I go over the bridge?
   **B:** No, go <u>under</u> the bridge.

3. **A:** Do I go up the steps?
   **B:** No, go <u>down</u> the steps.

4. **A:** Do I go past the bank?
   **B:** No, go past the <u>post office</u>.

**B** Listen again and repeat.

**C** Listen to the questions. Underline the stressed words in the answers.

1. No, take the <u>first</u> street on the right.
2. No, go past the supermarket.
3. No, go over the bridge.
4. No, go around the post office.

**D** Listen. Complete the questions. Then practice the conversations with a partner.

1. **A:** Do I take the _____ street on the _____?
   **B:** No, take the first street on the right.

2. **A:** Do I go _____ the _____?
   **B:** No, go past the supermarket.

## 3 Real-life math

**A** Read about Sara. Answer the question.

Sara can walk one mile in 20 minutes. The distance from the train station to the bank is 1/2 mile. How long will it take Sara to walk from the train station to the bank? _____

**B** How did you find the answer? Tell a partner.

*I divided…*

---

**TEST YOURSELF** ✓

Role-play a conversation about directions. Use the map in this unit or draw your own map. Partner A: Ask your partner for directions to a place. Partner B: Give your partner the directions. Then change roles.

## 1 Get ready to read

**A** **Read the definitions.**

be in the mood for: want to do something
make eye contact: look into a person's eyes
stranger: a person you don't know

smile

**B** **Where do you sometimes talk with strangers?**
**Check (✔) your answer(s).**

☐ at the bus stop    ☐ at the supermarket    ☐ at the doctor's office
☐ in a coffee shop    ☐ at parties    ☐ other: _____

## 2 Read about making small talk

**A** **Read the article. Where do people make small talk?**

### ◖ Small Talk

Small talk is everyday social conversation. Sometimes people make small talk with strangers, for example, at the bus stop, at the supermarket, or at the doctor's office. Students make small talk with their classmates before class starts. People also make small talk at parties.

For some people, small talk is very easy, but other people get nervous.[1] They don't know what to say. Sports, TV programs, and movies are good topics[2] for small talk. The weather is also a very good topic. People often begin a conversation with a statement about the weather. They say, for example, "It's a beautiful day," or, "It's freezing today."

Sometimes people don't want to talk. Maybe they are busy, or they are not in the mood for a conversation. Before you begin a conversation, make eye contact with the person. Wait for the person to look at you and smile. The smile says, "It's OK. Let's talk." Small talk is a good way to meet people and make friends.

Small talk at a party

[1] nervous: worried; a little upset
[2] topic: something you talk, write, or learn about

**B** **Listen and read the article again.**

**C** Mark the sentences T (true) or F (false).

_____ 1. People don't usually make small talk at parties.

_____ 2. Weather, sports, and movies are all good small talk topics.

_____ 3. People are always in the mood for conversation.

_____ 4. Small talk can help you make friends.

**D** Complete the sentences. Use the words in the box.

| topic    eye contact    smile    strangers |

1. Please give me an idea for a good _____ of conversation.

2. Some people don't like to talk to _____.

3. First make _____. Then you can begin a conversation.

4. Wait for a person to _____. Then say, "Good morning."

# 3 Read an invitation

**A** Read the invitation. Answer the questions.

## Potluck party for new students!

DATE:   September 21st
TIME:   7–9 p.m.
PLACE:  34 Crest Avenue, Highfield

## Bring your favorite food or drink.

1. Who is the party for? _The party is for new students._

2. Who will bring the food? _____

3. When will the party start? _____

4. Where will the party be? _____

**B** Think about the questions. Talk about the answers with your class.

1. Do you like to bring food to parties? Why or why not?

2. Does a party usually start on time?

3. What do you usually talk about at parties?

## BRING IT TO LIFE

Start a conversation in English with someone at school, at work, or in your neighborhood. Make small talk. Tell the class about your conversation.

## 1 Grammar

**A** Read the chart about Bianca and Tony's travel plans. Then answer the questions below.

|  | July | September | December |
|---|---|---|---|
| **Florida** |  |  | Bianca and Tony |
| **Illinois** | Tony |  |  |
| **California** |  | Bianca |  |

Chicago

1. Will Bianca and Tony go to Illinois in December? <u>No, they won't.</u>
2. Will Bianca go to California in July? _____
3. Will Tony go to Illinois in July? _____
4. Will Tony and Bianca go to Florida in December? _____

**B** Circle the correct words.

1. Ana always ( takes / will take ) her vacation in August.
2. The weather ( is / will be ) sunny tomorrow.
3. Next year I ( learn / will learn ) to drive.
4. They usually ( have / will have ) a music festival in July.

**C** Circle the correct words.

1. The movie starts ( on / at ) 6 p.m.
2. I'm going to Florida ( in / on ) December.
3. My birthday is ( on / at ) January 23rd.
4. January is ( before / after ) February.

> **Grammar note**
>
> **Prepositions of time**
> *at* + time          *in* + month
>    It's at 4 p.m.       It's in July.
>
> *on* + day/date
>    It's on Monday.
>    It's on July 23rd.

**D** Unscramble the questions.

1. she / to Chicago / go / will / when
   <u>When will she go to Chicago?</u>

2. this weekend / watch / Will / the game / they
   _____

3. Will / this winter / you / take / a vacation
   _____

4. we / Where / will / five years from now / be
   _____

## 2 Group work

**A** Work with 2–3 classmates. Use the map on page 22. Write a conversation between the people in the pictures. Share your conversation with the class.

A: *Hi, I'm at the corner of 1st Street and Park Avenue. How can I get to your house from here?*

B: *Well, first…*

**B** Choose one event in the box. Choose a date and time for it. Write it on the calendar. Then find 3 classmates who can go with you to the event at that time.

| concert | movie | party |
|---------|-------|-------|

A: *Hi, there's a baseball game on Saturday at 10 a.m. Can you go with me?*

B: *Yes, I can.*

**My weekend calendar**

|  | FRI. | SAT. | SUN. |
|---|------|------|------|
| 10 a.m. |  | baseball game |  |
| 3 p.m. |  |  |  |
| 8 p.m. |  |  |  |

**C** Talk about your calendar with the class.

## PROBLEM SOLVING

**A** Listen and read about Gina's problem.

Gina wants to go to the movies with a friend on Friday evening. The movie starts at 7:00 p.m. Gina works until 6:00 on Friday. Then she usually goes home and cooks dinner for her children. Gina's mother, Sofia, sometimes takes care of the children. But on Friday evenings, Sofia likes to stay home and watch her favorite TV program.

**B** Work with your classmates. Answer the questions.

1. What is Gina's problem?
2. What can she do? Think of 3 solutions to her problem.

# Moving Out

**FOCUS ON**

- household problems and repairs
- information about housing
- the comparative
- renting an apartment or a house
- where people live in the U.S.

## LESSON **1**  Vocabulary

### **1** Learn about common household problems

**A** Look at the pictures. Name the parts of the house.

  **B** Listen and look at the pictures.

 **C** Listen and repeat the words.

| | | |
|---|---|---|
| 1. dripping faucet | 3. leaking pipe | 5. no electricity |
| 2. broken door | 4. mice | 6. cracked window |

**D** Complete the sentences. Read the sentences to a partner.

1. There's _____no electricity_____ in the basement.
2. There's a _____ in the living room.
3. There's a _____ in the bathroom.
4. There's a _____ in the kitchen.
5. There's a _____ in the bedroom.
6. There are _____ in the garage.

☑ Identify household problems; recognize household maintenance

## 2 Talk about household repairs

**A** **Work with your classmates. Match the words with the pictures.**

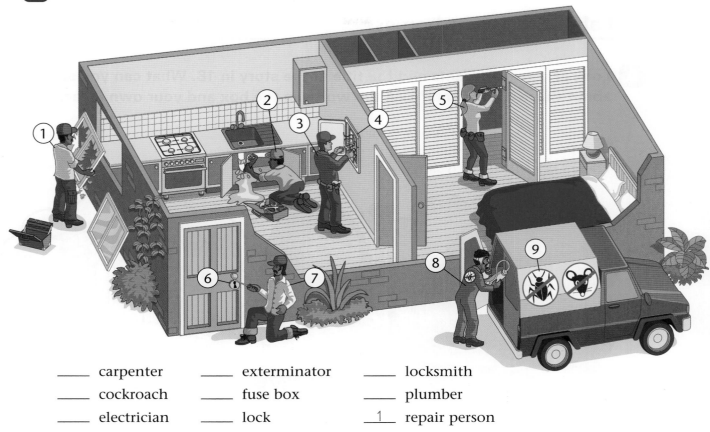

| | | |
|---|---|---|
| ____ carpenter | ____ exterminator | ____ locksmith |
| ____ cockroach | ____ fuse box | ____ plumber |
| ____ electrician | ____ lock | __1__ repair person |

**B** **Listen and check your answers. Then practice the words with a partner.**

**C** **Look at the picture. Complete the sentences.**

1. The _____ carpenter _____ is repairing the door.
2. The _____ is checking the fuse box.
3. The _____ is fixing the leaking pipe.
4. The _____ is fixing the broken window.
5. The _____ is fixing the lock on the front door.
6. The _____ is getting rid of the mice and cockroaches.

**D** **Interview a partner. Ask and answer the questions.**

1. Which repair jobs can you do?
2. Which jobs are easy? Which are difficult?

**TEST YOURSELF** ✔

Close your book. Write 5 household problems and 5 kinds of repair people. Check your spelling in a dictionary.

# 1 Read about different homes

**A** Look at the apartments and the title of the story in 1B. What can you say about these apartments? Use the words in the box and your own ideas.

| safe | dangerous | sunny | dark |

*Teresa's new apartment is sunny.*

Teresa's old apartment

Teresa's new apartment

 **B** Listen and read the story.

### Teresa's New Home

Teresa likes her new two-bedroom apartment. There are many windows, and it's very sunny. It's also near her children's school and a shopping center. Her apartment building is in a safe neighborhood.

Teresa's old apartment wasn't very sunny. It was too dark, and there weren't many windows. It was also smaller than the new apartment. There were a lot of problems with the old apartment. It was far from the children's school, and the neighborhood was too dangerous. Teresa is very happy in her new home.

**C** Check your understanding. Circle the correct words.

1. Teresa likes her new ( (home) / car ).
2. It has ( one / two ) bedrooms.
3. Her old apartment was ( sunny / far from the school ).
4. Her new apartment is in a ( safe / dangerous ) neighborhood.

**Grammar note**

***too* + adjective**
*too* = more than is good
It's too dark. I can't see.

## 2 Write about your dream home

**A** Think about your dream home. Answer the questions. Write your answers in a paragraph.

¹ Is your dream home a house or an apartment?  ² How many bedrooms does it have? ³ Is it near or far from a school?  ⁴ Is it a sunny place or a dark place?  ⁵ Is it in a safe neighborhood?  ⁶ How do you feel about your home?

_My dream home is_ _____

_____

_____

**B** Read your paragraph to a partner. How are your dream homes different?


# 3 Understand housing ads

**A** Listen to Anya describe her dream home. Circle the things she wants.

1. Number of bedrooms:   2  3  4
2. Number of bathrooms:  1  2  3
3. Near:   mall    school   bus stop
4. Rent:   $500   $800     $1,200

**B** Read the ad. Complete the sentences.

| security deposit | bathroom | evenings |
| manager | month | ~~large~~ |

FOR RENT: lg sunny 2BR 1BA apt, nr school and mall, $500/mo. $200 sec. dep. Call mgr eves at 555-5151.

1. It's a _____large_____ apartment with two bedrooms and one _____.
2. The rent is $500 a _____ and the _____ is $200.
3. For information, call the _____ at 555-5151 in the _____.

**C** Listen. Then practice the conversation with a partner. Use your own ideas.

A: Tell me about your dream home.
B: Well, I want three bedrooms.
A: Do you need a garage?
B: No, I don't.

**Need help?**

I want a…
   garage.
   family room.
   backyard.

**TEST YOURSELF** ✓

Close your book. Write a housing ad for your dream home. Read your ad to your partner.

## 1 Learn the comparative

**A** Look at the floor plans. Then listen and read about the apartments. What do you think? Which apartment is better?

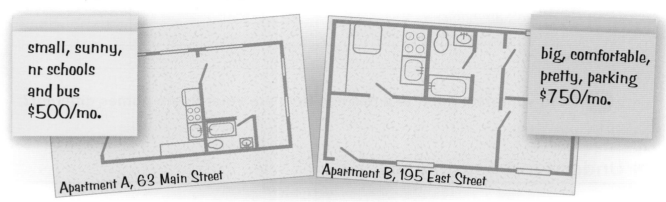

small, sunny, nr schools and bus $500/mo.

Apartment A, 63 Main Street

big, comfortable, pretty, parking $750/mo.

Apartment B, 195 East Street

Apartment A is smaller and cheaper than apartment B, and it's more convenient. Apartment A is very sunny. Apartment B is bigger and more comfortable. It's also a very pretty apartment, but it's more expensive.

**B** Study the chart. Write the comparative forms of the adjectives below.

### THE COMPARATIVE

|  | Adjective | Comparative | Notes |
|---|---|---|---|
| One syllable | small<br>large<br>big | smaller<br>larger<br>bigger | Add -er or -r.<br>For words like *big* and *hot*,<br>double the final consonant. |
| Ending in -y | sunny | sunnier | Change *y* to *i* and add -er. |
| Two or more syllables | convenient | more convenient | Put *more* in front of the adjective. |
| Irregular forms | good<br>bad | better<br>worse | |

1. hot ___hotter___    3. sunny _____    5. bad _____

2. nice _____    4. expensive _____    6. good _____

**C** Complete the sentences. Use the comparative of the words in parentheses.

1. Apartment A is _____cheaper than_____ apartment B. (cheap)

2. Apartment B is _____ apartment A. (pretty)

3. Apartment B is _____ apartment A. (comfortable)

## 2 Ask and answer questions with *Which*

**A** Study the charts. Practice the questions and answers.

| Questions with *Which* | Answers |
|---|---|
| Which is better, apartment A or apartment B?<br>Which apartment is better, A or B? | Apartment A is better than apartment B. *or*<br>Apartment A is. |

**B** Complete the questions. Then answer the questions with your opinion. Use the comparative.

1. Which is usually _____cheaper_____, an apartment or a house? (cheap)

   _I think an apartment is usually cheaper than a house._

2. Which place is _____, a small town or a big city? (safe)

   _____

3. Which is _____, a car or a bicycle? (dangerous)

   _____

4. Which city is _____, New York or San Francisco? (expensive)

   _____

## 3 Practice using the comparative

**A** Read the questions. Write your answers in your notebook. Use the words in the box and your own ideas.

| quiet | comfortable | convenient | safe | noisy | warm | pretty | cheap |
|---|---|---|---|---|---|---|---|

1. Which is better, a new house or an old house? Why?
2. Which is better, a small house or a large apartment? Why?
3. Which is better, an apartment on the first floor or on the top floor? Why?

**B** Interview a partner. Ask and answer the questions in 3A.

A: *Which is better, a new house or an old house?*
B: *I think a new house is better. It's more comfortable.*

**C** Talk about the answers with your class.

---

**TEST YOURSELF** ✔

Write 3 sentences about your partner's opinions in 3B.
*My partner thinks a new house is more comfortable than an old house.*

## 1 Learn how to ask questions about an apartment

**A** **Read the ad. Work with a partner. Ask and answer the questions.**

1. How many bedrooms does the apartment have?
2. Is it near a school?
3. How much is the rent?
4. Is there a security deposit?
5. Are utilities included?

> **For rent:** cozy 1BR 1BA apt, top floor, nr sch, $500/mo. $250 sec. dep. Parking space. Utils. incl. Call 219-555-4609.

**B** **Listen and read.**

**Sharon:** Hello. I'm calling about the apartment. How much is the rent?
**Manager:** It's $600 a month plus utilities.
**Sharon:** Is there a security deposit?
**Manager:** Yes, there is. It's $350.
**Sharon:** When will the apartment be available?
**Manager:** It'll be available on March 1st.

**C** **Listen again and repeat.**

**D** **Work with a partner. Practice the conversation. Use the questions in 1A and your own ideas.**

**E** **Listen to Sharon call about other apartments. Complete the notes.**

① **114 Maple St.**

Rent: _____ $600 _____

Deposit: _____

Utilities included:

   Yes / No

Available: _____

② **15 Center St.**

Rent: _____

Deposit: _____

Utilities included:

   Yes / No

Available: _____

③ **198 Second Ave.**

Rent: _____

Deposit: _____

Utilities included:

   Yes / No

Available: _____

## 2 Practice your pronunciation

 **A** **Listen to the falling and rising intonation. Then listen again and repeat.**

INFORMATION QUESTIONS

How much is the rent? ↘

When is the apartment available? ↘

YES/NO QUESTIONS

Does it include utilities? ↗

Is there a parking garage? ↗

 **B** **Read the questions. Check (✔) *Falling* or *Rising*. Then listen and check your answers.**

|  | Falling ↘ | Rising ↗ |
|---|---|---|
| 1. When can I see it? | ✔ | |
| 2. Is there a garage? | | ✔ |
| 3. Is it near the bank? | | |
| 4. How much is the rent? | | |
| 5. What's the address? | | |
| 6. Is it sunny? | | |

**C** **Work with a partner. Practice the questions. Use falling and rising intonation.**

## 3 Real-life math

**A** **Read the information about Antonio's new apartment. Answer the questions.**

1. How much will Antonio pay on June 1st?

   _____

2. How much will Antonio spend on rent in one year? (Don't add the deposit.)

   _____

> **RENTAL AGREEMENT**
> Rent per month: $600
> Deposit: $300
> First month's rent and deposit
>   due on: June 1st
> Signature: Antonio Lopez

**B** **How did you find the answers? Tell a partner.**

*First I added. Then I multiplied…*

---

**TEST YOURSELF** ✓

Role-play a conversation about an apartment. Use information from an ad in this unit. Partner A: You want to rent an apartment. Partner B: You have an apartment for rent. Then change roles.

## 1 Get ready to read

**A** Read the definitions.

crowded: many people in a small space

less: the opposite of more

population: the number of people in a city, state, or country

**B** Answer the questions.

1. Does your city or town have a large population?
2. Does your state have a large population?

## 2 Read about the population in the U.S.

**A** Read the article.

### Small Town or BIG CITY?

The United States has a population of more than 295 million people. The East and West Coasts are very crowded. For example, in the West, there are more than 10 million people in the area of Los Angeles, California. In the East, there are more than 21 million people in and around New York City. The eastern state of New Jersey has more than 1,000 people per[1] square mile!

Areas in the center of the country are usually less crowded. For example, the state of Wyoming has only 500,000 people. That is only 5.1 people per square mile.

Many people are looking for the "perfect" place to live. Some people love big city life,

[1] per: for each
[2] tiny: very small

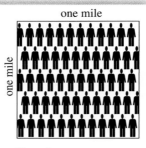

Wyoming: 5 people per square mile

New Jersey: more than 1,000 people per square mile

but it is usually more expensive. Some people think life in a small town is better. Small towns are quieter and less crowded. Some small towns have populations of 10,000 to 15,000 people—like Grants Pass, Oregon, or the town of Owasso, Oklahoma. Some people want a really small town. For those people, there's the tiny[2] town of Harmony, California. Population? 18!

STUDENT AUDIO

**B** Listen and read the article again.

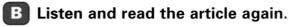
☑ Interpret information about U.S. population; interpret maps

**C** Mark the statements T (true) or F (false).

_____ 1. There are more than 21 million people in the New York area.

_____ 2. Wyoming is more crowded than New Jersey.

_____ 3. Life in a big city is usually more expensive than life in a small town.

_____ 4. Grants Pass, Oregon, is smaller than Harmony, California.

**D** Complete the sentences. Use the words in the box.

| crowded | less | population | square mile |
|---|---|---|---|

1. The _____ of the U.S. is more than 295 million.

2. Some cities in the U.S. are getting very _____.

3. Wyoming has 5.1 people per _____.

4. Small towns are usually _____ crowded than big cities.

## 3 Read a population map

**A** Look at the map. Answer the questions.

1. Which state has more people, Minnesota or Oregon?

2. Which state has a population of less than two million, Florida or New Mexico?

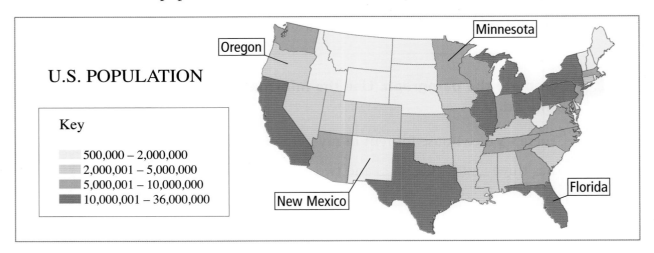

U.S. POPULATION

Key

500,000 – 2,000,000
2,000,001 – 5,000,000
5,000,001 – 10,000,000
10,000,001 – 36,000,000

Oregon    Minnesota    New Mexico    Florida

**B** Think about the questions. Talk about the answers with your class.

1. What area of the country do you want to live in?

2. Why are big cities usually more expensive than small towns?

**BRING IT TO LIFE**

Find information about the population of your town, city, or state in the library or on the Internet. Talk about the information with your class.

## 1 Grammar

**A** Write the comparative forms in the chart.

| Adjectives | Comparative | Adjectives | Comparative |
|---|---|---|---|
| small | smaller | hot | |
| nice | | noisy | |
| good | | bad | |
| expensive | | convenient | |

**B** Complete the questions. Then write your opinion. Use the comparative.

1. Which is _____more expensive_____, an apartment or a house? (expensive)
   _I think a house is usually more expensive than an apartment._

2. Which is _____, a book or a movie? (exciting)
   _____

3. Which is _____, a bus or a train? (convenient)
   _____

4. Which is _____, a small town or a big city? (safe)
   _____

**C** Complete the paragraph. Use the information in the ad.

> House for rent: 3BR 2BA, lg yard, $1,300/mo., $500 sec. dep. Util. not incl. Call mgr eves at 555-4326.

There's a nice house for rent in my neighborhood.

It has three ___bedrooms___ and two _____.
                    1                              2
There's a _____ yard behind the house. The rent is $1,300 a _____,
                3                                                              4
and the _____ is $500. The _____ are not included. You can
              5                              6
call the _____ in the _____ at 555-4326.
                      7                                    8

**D** Complete the sentences with *too* + adjective. Use the words in the box.

| old | ~~dangerous~~ | cold | dark |

1. Don't walk on this street. It's _____too dangerous_____.
2. I can't see. It's _____ in this room.
3. Don't buy that car. It's _____.
4. I need a sweater. It's _____ in here.

## 2 Group work

**A** Work with 2–3 classmates. Write 6 sentences about the apartments in the ads. Read your sentences to the class.

*The apartment on South Street is larger than the apartment on Pine Street.*

458 South Street, sunny 2BR apt, 4th floor, lg rooms, Util. incl., $700/mo.
Call 457-555-6334

43 Pine Street, 1BR apt, 1st floor, Util. extra, great neighborhood, nr shopping and theaters, $1,200/mo.
Call 457-555-4394

**B** Interview 3 classmates about their dream homes. Write their answers in the chart.

| Questions | Classmate 1 | Classmate 2 | Classmate 3 |
|---|---|---|---|
| 1.  Is your dream home in a big city? | | | |
| 2.  How many rooms does it have? | | | |
| 3.  How many bedrooms does it have? | | | |
| 4.  Does it have a backyard? | | | |
| 5.  Does it have _____? | | | |

**C** Talk about the answers with your class.

### PROBLEM SOLVING

**A** Listen and read about Dan and Lia's problem.

Dan and Lia are renting an apartment in the city. It is very expensive. They want to buy a house, but houses in the city are more expensive than apartments. Houses in the small town of Riverville are less expensive.

Right now Dan and Lia don't have the money for a house in the city. But they have the money for a house in Riverville. Dan works in the city. From Riverville, he will have to travel two hours by car to work every day.

**B** Work with your classmates. Answer the questions.

1.  What is Dan and Lia's problem?
2.  What should they do? Think of 2 or 3 solutions to their problem.

# UNIT 4

# Looking for Work

**FOCUS ON**
- jobs and job applications
- job interviews and ads
- the simple past
- job histories
- career goals

## LESSON 1  Vocabulary

### 1 Learn words for job applications

**A** Look at Katia's job application. Name 2 things you know about her.

**B** Listen and look at the sections of the job application.

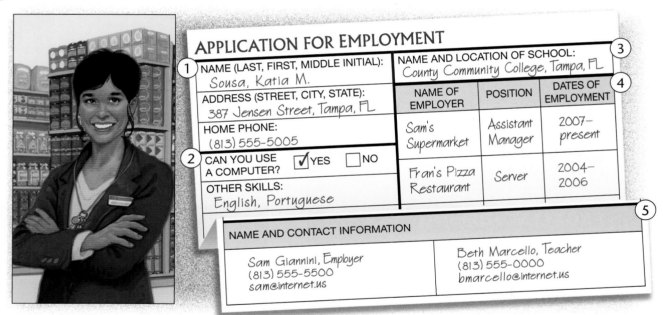

APPLICATION FOR EMPLOYMENT

1. NAME (LAST, FIRST, MIDDLE INITIAL):
Sousa, Katia M.

ADDRESS (STREET, CITY, STATE):
387 Jensen Street, Tampa, FL

HOME PHONE:
(813) 555-5005

2. CAN YOU USE A COMPUTER?  ☑YES  ☐NO

OTHER SKILLS:
English, Portuguese

3. NAME AND LOCATION OF SCHOOL:
County Community College, Tampa, FL

| NAME OF EMPLOYER | POSITION | DATES OF EMPLOYMENT |
|---|---|---|
| Sam's Supermarket | Assistant Manager | 2007– present |
| Fran's Pizza Restaurant | Server | 2004– 2006 |

4.

NAME AND CONTACT INFORMATION

Sam Giannini, Employer
(813) 555-5500
sam@internet.us

Beth Marcello, Teacher
(813) 555-0000
bmarcello@internet.us

5.

**C** Listen and repeat the words.

1. personal information
2. job skills
3. education
4. employment history
5. references

**D** Complete the sentences. Read the sentences to a partner.

1. Katia writes the name of her manager at Sam's in the _____references_____ section.

2. Katia writes her languages in the _____ section.

3. The name of Katia's college goes in the _____ section.

4. Katia's name and address are in the _____ section.

5. Katia's last job is in the _____ section.

☑ Identify common jobs; identify job application vocabulary

## 2 Talk about jobs

**A** Work with your classmates. Match the words with the pictures.

_____ accountant       _____ job applicant       _____ mover

_____ chef       __1__ job counselor       _____ sales clerk

_____ computer programmer       _____ mail carrier       _____ veterinarian

**B** Listen and check your answers. Then practice the words with a partner.

**C** Complete the sentences.

1. A _____ _mover_ _____ brings furniture to a new home.
2. An _____ helps people with their taxes.
3. A _____ cooks food in a restaurant.
4. A _____ takes care of sick animals.
5. A _____ writes new computer programs.
6. A _____ delivers mail.
7. A _____ helps customers in a store.
8. A job counselor talks with a _____ about jobs.

**D** Interview a partner. Ask and answer the questions.

1. Which of the jobs on this page are interesting to you? Why?
2. Which is more important for a job, education or experience?

**TEST YOURSELF** ✓

Close your book. Write 5 job application terms and 5 jobs. Check your spelling in a dictionary.

# 1 Read about job interviews

**A** Look at the pictures and the title of the story in 1B. What do you think? Will Adam get the job?

**B** Listen and read the story.

### Adam's Job Interviews

Adam is looking for a job. He goes to job interviews every week. Before the interview, he looks for some information about the company. He also writes some questions: for example, "What will I do?" He always wears nice clothes like a suit or pants with a shirt and tie. He looks clean and neat.

He's sometimes late for interviews, and he usually feels nervous. When he shakes hands, he doesn't make eye contact with the interviewer. He answers all of the questions, but he doesn't smile very much. Adam is confused. He had an interview last week. He felt nervous, but he answered all the questions. He had the right experience and job skills. Why didn't he get the job?

**C** Check your understanding. Adam makes 3 mistakes at job interviews. Check (✔) the mistakes.

- ☐ 1. He writes questions for the job interview.
- ☐ 2. He wears nice clothes.
- ☑ 3. He's sometimes late for interviews.
- ☐ 4. He doesn't look at the interviewer.
- ☐ 5. He answers all of the questions.
- ☐ 6. He doesn't smile very much.

## 2 Write about a job interview

**A** Think about a job interview. Answer the questions. Write your answers in a paragraph.

¹ What do you do before a job interview?  ² What do you wear to the interview?
³ Do you arrive late or on time?  ⁴ How do you feel?  ⁵ Do you like to go to job interviews?

_____

Before a job interview, I _____

_____

_____

**Need help?**

I feel...
   cheerful.
   worried.
   confident.
   happy.
   nervous.

**B** Read your paragraph to a partner. Does your partner like interviews?

## 3 Interpret a job ad

**A** Listen. Check (✔) the correct information about each job.

| Job | Part-time | Full-time | References required |
|-----|-----------|-----------|---------------------|
| Chef |  |  |  |
| Sales clerk |  |  |  |

**B** Read the job ad. Complete the sentences. Use the words in the box.

| part-time    experience    immediately    references |

WANTED:
Assistant breakfast chef, p/t 6 a.m.–10 a.m., exp. and written refs required, start immed.

1. The hours are from 6 a.m. to 10 a.m. It's a _____ job.
2. You need written _____ for this job.
3. _____ is also required.
4. They need someone right now. The job starts _____.

**C** Listen. Then practice the conversation with a partner. Use your own ideas.

A: I want to work at the front desk in a hotel.
B: What skills do you need for that job?
A: I need to speak English and know how to use a computer.

**Need help?**

I want to...
   work at the front desk in a hotel.
   be an accountant.

**TEST YOURSELF** ✓

Close your book. Write 2 things you should do and 2 things you shouldn't do before and during an interview. Tell a partner.

## 1 Learn the simple past

**A** Listen and read about Katia. Did she work and study at the same time?

In 2004, Katia Sousa worked at Fran's Pizza Restaurant. Every evening, she went to community college and took classes in Business Administration and English. She graduated in 2006. Then she got a job at Sam's Supermarket as an assistant manager. Last week, she applied for a job at State Bank.

**B** Study the charts. Complete the sentences below.

### THE SIMPLE PAST

| Affirmative statements | | | | | | | | Verbs |
|---|---|---|---|---|---|---|---|---|

**Affirmative statements**

| I / You / He / She | worked | at Sam's. | We / You / They | worked | at Sam's. |
|---|---|---|---|---|---|

**Verbs**

**Regular**
work — worked
apply — applied

**Irregular**
do — did
eat — ate
get — got
go — went
have — had
make — made
read — read
take — took
write — wrote

1. He _____ at Sam's.    2. They _____ at Sam's.

**Negative statements**

| I / You / He / She | didn't work | at Sam's. | We / You / They | didn't work | at Sam's. |
|---|---|---|---|---|---|

3. You _____ work at Sam's.    4. We didn't _____ at Sam's.

**C** Complete the sentences. Use the simple past of the verbs.

AFFIRMATIVE

1. Katia _____worked_____ at Sam's Supermarket in 2006. (work)
2. She _____ to County Community College. (go)
3. She _____ English classes. (take)

NEGATIVE

4. She _____didn't take_____ Portuguese classes. (take)
5. She _____ in 2005. (graduate)
6. She _____ a job interview at a school. (have)

# 2 Ask and answer *Yes/No* questions in the simple past

**A** Study the chart. Complete the questions and answers below.

| Yes/No questions and short answers | | |
|---|---|---|
| **A:** Did you work at Sam's?<br>**B:** Yes, I did. | **A:** Did she work at the bank?<br>**B:** No, she didn't. | **A:** Did they take English?<br>**B:** No, they didn't. |

1. **A:** _____ you work at Sam's?
   **B:** Yes, I _____ .

2. **A:** Did they _____ English?
   **B:** No, they _____ .

**B** Look at the list. What did Katia do yesterday?
Answer the questions. (✔ = yes, X = no)

1. Did Katia have breakfast? _No, she didn't._
2. Did she go to the interview? _____
3. Did she write an email to the interviewer? _____
4. Did Katia and Jack eat dinner at Fran's? _____

*Yesterday:*
*X have breakfast*
*✓ go to the*
*interview at*
*State Bank*
*X write an email to*
*the interviewer*
*✓ eat dinner with*
*Jack at Fran's*

**C** Circle the correct words.

1. Did Sue and Ron ( go / went ) to the baseball game?
2. No, they ( go / went ) to a movie.
3. Did they ( like / liked ) the movie?
4. Yes, they ( like / liked ) it very much.

# 3 Practice asking *Yes/No* questions about the past

**A** What did you do yesterday? Check (✔) *Yes* or *No* in the chart.

| Did you... | Yes | No | Did you... | Yes | No |
|---|---|---|---|---|---|
| go to work? | | | go to a party? | | |
| read the newspaper? | | | write an email? | | |

**B** Work with a partner. Ask and answer the questions in the chart.

**A:** *Did you go to work yesterday?*
**B:** *Yes, I did.*

**C** Talk about the answers with your class.

**TEST YOURSELF** ✔

Write 6 sentences about you and your partner. Use the information in 3A and 3B.
*I read the newspaper yesterday. My partner didn't go to a party.*

## 1 Learn how to answer job interview questions

**A** Read the information about each person. Answer the questions.

1. Did Mark graduate from college?  2. What are Min-hee's special skills?

|  | **Mark** | **Min-hee** |
|---|---|---|
| **Job wanted** | Office assistant | Dental assistant |
| **Education** | High school, computer training | 2 years college, accounting classes |
| **Experience** | 6 months at Energy Electrical Co. | 5 years in a dentist's office |
| **Special skills** | Good at math, computers | Good with children, speaks Korean |
| **References** | Joe Russo, Energy Electrical Co. | Dr. Jack Stone, dental office |

**B** Listen and read.

Interviewer: Tell me about your education.
Mark: Well, I finished high school, and I took some computer classes.
Interviewer: How much experience do you have?
Mark: I worked at Energy Electrical Company for six months.
Interviewer: Do you have any special skills?
Mark: I'm good at math! And I can use computers.
Interviewer: Do you have any references?
Mark: Yes, I do. My boss at Energy Electrical, Joe Russo, will give me a reference.

> **Grammar note**
>
> *to be good at (doing) something*
>
> I'm good at math.
> She's good at languages.
> We're good at using computers.

**C** Listen again and repeat.

**D** Work with a partner. Practice the conversation. Use Min-hee's information in 1A.

**E** Listen to 3 conversations. Match the conversations with the pictures.

_____ car salesperson   _____ mail carrier   _____ accountant

# 2 Practice your pronunciation

**A** Listen to the verbs in the simple present and simple past. How many syllables are there in each verb?

1. talk    talked
2. answer    answered
3. count    counted
4. want    wanted

**Need help?**

Regular verbs that end in the sound *t* or *d* have an extra syllable in the simple past.
For example, *wanted* sounds like *wan-ted*.

**B** Listen to the simple present and simple past of the verbs. How many syllables are there in the simple past?
Circle *1* or *2*.

1. clean    cleaned    (1) 2
2. need    needed    1  2
3. wait    waited    1  2

4. fix    fixed    1  2
5. check    checked    1  2
6. paint    painted    1  2

**C** Listen again and repeat.

**D** Read the sentences to a partner.

1. I cleaned the car.
2. She wanted a new job.

3. The carpenter fixed the door.
4. He painted the house in 2006.

# 3 Real-life math

**A** Work with a partner. Ask and answer questions about Matt's employment history.

A: *How long did Matt work at Cell Phone Center?*
B: *He worked there for 2 years and 9 months.*

> **Matt Rustigan**
> Tel: (317) 555-9654 • mattrustigan@internet.us
>
> **Employment History**
> Arena Events Company          March 1, 2006–February 28, 2009
> Sports Advertising Agency     November 1, 2004–February 28, 2006
> Cell Phone Center             February 1, 2002–October 31, 2004

**B** How much work experience does Matt have? What is the total in years and months?

**TEST YOURSELF** ✔

Role-play a job interview. Partner A: Your partner wants a job at your supermarket. Ask questions about his or her education and experience. Partner B: You want a job at a supermarket. Answer your partner's questions. Then change roles.

## 1 Get ready to read

**A** **Read the definitions.**

associate's degree: 2-year college diploma
bachelor's degree: 4-year college diploma
GED certificate: the same as a high school diploma
salary: money you get from work

Department of Education
**General Education Development**
High School Equivalency Certificate

Paul A. Butterfield

**B** **What do you think? Which jobs need more than a GED certificate or high school diploma?**

- [ ] accountant
- [ ] chef
- [ ] computer programmer
- [ ] mail carrier
- [ ] veterinary assistant

## 2 Read about jobs and education

**A** **Read the article. Where does Susan want to work?**

# Set a Career Goal

Education can help people get better jobs with better salaries. But education requires a lot of time and can cost a lot of money. First, it's important to set career[1] goals. Then you can plan for the education you will need.

Susan's career goal was to work in a hotel as an accountant. She is good at math, and she likes hotels. She made a plan and followed it step by step:

- She got her GED certificate.

- She got an associate's degree in Hotel and Restaurant Management.
- She worked as a desk clerk in a hotel and studied part-time. After three years, she got her bachelor's degree.
- Finally, she got a job in the accounting department[2] at the hotel.

It takes time, but it is important to set career goals and plan your education. Follow your plan. Then you can reach your career goal.

[1] career: a job (or jobs) you do for a long time; your working life
[2] accounting department: the area where accountants work

STUDENT
AUDIO

 **B** **Listen and read the article again.**

☑ Identify career goals; interpret a job training chart

**C** Mark the sentences T (true) or F (false).

_T_ 1. Education can help you get a job with a better salary.

_____ 2. You should get an education first. Then set your career goals.

_____ 3. Susan's goal was to be a front desk manager.

_____ 4. Susan got an associate's degree in Business Administration.

_____ 5. She worked at the hotel and studied part-time.

**D** Complete the sentences. Use the words in the box.

| career   ~~bachelor's~~   salary   associate's   GED certificate |

1. Most _____bachelor's_____ degrees require four years of college or university studies.

2. The _____ is the same as a high school diploma.

3. Susan's goal is to have a _____ as an accountant.

4. Susan studied Hotel Management and got an _____ degree.

5. More education can help a person get a higher _____.

# 3 Read a job training chart

**A** Look at the chart. Ask and answer questions about the chart.

| Position | Education/Training |
|---|---|
| Mail carrier | High school diploma or GED certificate |
| Assistant chef | High school diploma or GED certificate + 1 year on-the-job training |
| Veterinary assistant | Associate's degree + 1–2 years on-the-job training |
| Computer programmer | Bachelor's degree + 2 years on-the-job training |

A: *How much education and training does a mail carrier need?*
B: *A mail carrier needs…*

**B** Think about the questions. Talk about the answers with your class.

1. What things are important to you in a job? Money? Work you enjoy? Friendly co-workers? A good schedule?

2. What educational opportunities are there in your community?

**BRING IT TO LIFE**

Find out the education you need for your dream job. Search the Internet or go to the library. Talk about your education and career goals with the class.

## 1 Grammar

**A** Write the simple past of the irregular verbs in the chart.

| Verb | Simple past | Verb | Simple past |
|------|-------------|------|-------------|
| make |             | read |             |
| do   |             | eat  |             |
| go   |             | write|             |
| have |             | get  |             |

**B** Complete the sentences. Use the simple past of the verbs in parentheses.

1. Brigitte _____*studied*_____ math in college. (study)
2. She _____ Korean classes. (not take)
3. She _____ in a library. (work)
4. She _____ her job in the library. (not like)
5. She _____ for a job in a hotel. (apply)

> **Grammar note**
>
> **Simple past**
> For verbs that end in -*y,*
> change *y* to *i* and add -*ed.*
>     study → studied
>     apply → applied

**C** Write *Yes/No* questions and short answers. Use the simple past.

1. Sam / sleep late / this morning
   A: _Did Sam sleep late this morning_?
   B: No, he ____*didn't*____.

2. Antonia / go to a job interview / last week
   A: _____?
   B: No, she _____.

3. they / go to a meeting / this morning
   A: _____?
   B: Yes, they _____.

4. you / take / a math class
   A: _____?
   B: Yes, I _____.

**D** Complete the questions. Use the verbs in parentheses.

1. What time _____ you _____ to work yesterday? (go)
2. Where _____ they _____ lunch yesterday? (have)
3. When _____ Maria _____ from high school? (graduate)
4. What skills _____ he _____ for the job? (need)

> **Grammar note**
>
> **Simple past: information questions**
>
> | Where When | did | you he they | eat lunch? |
> |------------|-----|-------------|------------|

## 2 Group work

**A** Work with 2–3 classmates. Write a conversation between the people in the picture. Share your conversation with the class.

A: *Good morning. I have your job application. Now, tell me more about your education.*

B: *Well, I finished...*

**B** Interview 3 classmates. Write their answers in your notebook.

1. When did you get up yesterday?
2. Where did you go in the morning?
3. What did you do in the afternoon?
4. Did you have a good day?
5. What did you learn yesterday?

**C** Talk about the answers with your class.

## PROBLEM SOLVING

**A** Listen and read about Jin's problem.

Jin is married and has two young children. He works during the day, and he studies at the community college at night. Right now, he is taking three classes at the college. He goes to school three nights every week. He works from 8:00 in the morning to 5:00 in the evening, Monday to Friday. He also has a lot of homework to do on the weekends. Jin is frustrated. He says, "I want an education. I want to get a better job, but I'm very tired. I never see my family."

**B** Work with your classmates. Answer the questions.

1. What is Jin's problem?
2. What can he do? Think of 2 or 3 solutions to his problem.

# On the Job

**FOCUS ON**
- pay stubs and the workplace
- workplace behavior
- *might* and *might not*
- directions on the job
- job performance and evaluation

**LESSON 1** Vocabulary

## 1 Learn to read a pay stub

**A** Look at the pay stub. What is the name of the company?

**B** Listen and look at the pay stub.

| ① PAY PERIOD |
| --- |
| 01/10/08–01/16/08 |

**Mills Brothers Company**

| EMPLOYEE NAME | SSN | EMPLOYEE NUMBER |
| --- | --- | --- |
| Pablo Ramirez | 123-45-6789 | 0005643 |

**EARNINGS**

| | | |
| --- | --- | --- |
| Hours | 28 | |
| ② Hourly rate | $15.25 | |
| ③ Gross pay | | $427.00 |
| ④ Deductions | | -$ 93.00 |
| ⑤ Net pay | | $334.00 |

**DEDUCTIONS**

| | |
| --- | --- |
| State tax | $19.10 |
| ⑥ Federal tax | $42.70 |
| ⑦ Medicare | $ 6.20 |
| ⑧ Social Security | $25.00 |
| Total deductions | $93.00 |

**C** Listen and repeat the words.

1. pay period   3. gross pay   5. net pay   7. Medicare
2. hourly rate   4. deductions   6. federal tax   8. Social Security

**D** Complete the sentences. Read the sentences to a partner.

1. Pablo's net pay is his gross pay minus the _____deductions_____.
2. The deduction for _____ is $25.
3. Pablo's _____ is $15.25 per hour.
4. The deduction for _____ is $42.70.
5. Pablo's _____ for this week is $427.
6. This _____ is one week.
7. Pablo paid $6.20 for _____.

## 2 Talk about workplace machines

**A** **Work with your classmates. Match the words with the picture.**

| | | |
|---|---|---|
| ____ computer | ____ forklift | ____ scanner |
| _1_ fax machine | ____ photocopier | ____ time clock |
| ____ file cabinet | ____ printer | ____ vending machine |

**B** **Listen and check your answers. Then practice the words with a partner.**

**C** **Look at the picture. Complete the sentences.**

1. The ___photocopier___ is next to the file cabinet.
2. The _____ is on the wall.
3. The _____ is to the left of the computer.
4. The _____ is to the right of the computer.
5. The _____ is between the door and the window.
6. The _____ is on the small table.
7. The _____ is in the deliveries area.

**D** **Work with a partner. Practice the conversation. Use the picture in 2A.**

A: Where is the photocopier?
B: It's next to the file cabinet.

**E** **Interview a partner. Ask and answer the questions.**

1. Which workplace machines do you have at home, at work, or at school?
2. Where are they?

**TEST YOURSELF** ✔

Close your book. Write 5 words from the pay stub and 5 workplace machines. Check your spelling in a dictionary.

# 1 Read about workplace behavior

**A** Look at the pictures and the title of the story in 1B. Guess the answers to the questions.

1. What does Lucy do?
2. Does she like her job?

 **B** Listen and read the story.

## Lucy's New Job

I started my new job three weeks ago. I work as a sandwich chef at the deli counter in the supermarket. I start work at 7 a.m. every day, and I have to be on time for work. On the first day, I learned about the important health and safety rules for this job. We have to keep our hands and tools clean. We also have to wear appropriate clothing. I wear a white jacket and a hairnet. My hair is very long, and it might get into the food! I have to use plastic gloves to prepare the food.

I work on a team with a salad chef and a cashier. I like to talk to the customers. I always smile and say, "Have a nice day!" I'm very happy with my new job.

**C** Check your understanding. Circle *a* or *b*.

1. Lucy is a _____.
   a. cashier
   b. sandwich chef

2. Lucy wears a _____.
   a. white jacket
   b. white hat

3. Lucy _____ to talk to the customers.
   a. likes
   b. doesn't like

## 2 Write about work or school

**A** Think about your job, your English class, or another class. Complete the paragraph.

**Need help?**

I wear...
 a hard hat.
 a suit.
 safety glasses.
 a uniform.

_____

I started my _____ _____ ago. I _____
                 (job/class)                              (work as a/study)

at _____. Every day I start at _____. On the first day,

we learned about _____. _____, I usually
                                              (In class/At work)

wear _____ and _____. I sometimes talk

to _____. I am _____ with my _____.
                              (happy/not happy)                (job/class)

**B** Read your paragraph to a partner. What does your partner usually wear to work or class?

## 3 Identify appropriate job behavior

**A** Listen to the conversation. Check (✔) the types of work behavior you hear.

✔ Be on time for work.     ☐ Follow safety rules.

☐ Listen carefully to instructions.     ☐ Ask for help.

☐ Wear appropriate clothing.     ☐ Smile when you talk to customers.

**B** Listen. Then practice the conversation with a partner. Use your own ideas.

A: Could you tell me about the school dress code?

B: Well, you have to wear appropriate clothing. You can't wear shorts or T-shirts.

A: Are there any other rules?

B: Yes, there are. You can't eat or drink near the computers.

**Need help?**

You can't...
 smoke
 listen to music
 make phone calls

**C** Work with a partner. Make a list of rules for your classroom.

_We have to speak English in class._

**TEST YOURSELF** ✔

Close your book. Write 2 things you have to do and 2 things you can't do in your class or in your workplace. Tell a partner.

## 1 Learn *might* and *might not*

**A** Listen and read the conversation. Answer the questions.

1. Who wants to see Martin?
2. Was Martin on time for work?

**Martin:** I was late for work today. The boss might be angry with me. I might get fired!

**Akiko:** Don't worry. He might not be angry. You worked very hard last month. He might give you a raise!

MEMO
Re: PAY RAISE
MARTIN R.
$10.50 ► $12.00

Martin R.

**B** Study the charts.

### *MIGHT* AND *MIGHT NOT*

| Affirmative statements | | | Negative statements | | | Note |
|---|---|---|---|---|---|---|
| I<br>You<br>He<br>She<br>We<br>They | might | be angry.<br>get fired.<br>get a raise. | I<br>You<br>He<br>She<br>We<br>They | might not | be angry.<br>get fired.<br>get a raise. | We use *might* to say that something is possible. |

**C** Complete the sentences. Use *might (not)* and the words in the box.

| make a mistake | get a raise | be at work today | ~~get to work on time~~ |
|---|---|---|---|

1. There's a lot of traffic this morning.
   I _might not get to work on time_ .

2. Lea worked very hard this year.
   She _____ .

3. Aaron didn't read the instructions carefully.
   He _____ .

4. Sofia didn't answer the phone in her office.
   She _____ .

## 2 Statements with *might* and *should*

**Complete the sentences. Use *should* or *might*.**

1. **A:** I feel sick.

   **B:** You ___should___ go home early today.

2. **A:** The floor is wet.

   **B:** Yes, we _____ be careful.

3. **A:** What's this deduction for?

   **B:** I don't know. It _____ be for Medicare or Social Security.

4. **A:** Where's Lucy?

   **B:** I'm not sure. She _____ be at lunch. She's not at her desk.

5. **A:** I'm so sleepy.

   **B:** Then you _____ go to bed early tonight.

> **Grammar note**
>
> **Review: *should***
>
> I
> You  } should go home.
> They
>
> We use *should* to say that something is a good idea.

## 3 Practice using *might* and *should*

**A** **Look at the pictures. Write 2 things each person might do. Write 2 things they should do.**

*He might run out of the store.*
*He should mop the floor.*

**B** **Work with a partner. Talk about the pictures.**

**A:** *What do you think this person might do?*
**B:** *I think she might go home.*

**C** **Talk about the answers with your class.**

---

**TEST YOURSELF** ✔

Close your book. Write sentences about 2 things that you might do tomorrow and 2 things your partner might do. Read your sentences to a partner.

## **1 Learn how to understand and clarify job instructions**

**A** Look at the pictures. Which things can you do?

make photocopies   operate a forklift   scan documents   send a fax   type a letter

**B** Listen and read.

**Rachel:**   John, could you type this letter for me, please?

**John:**   Of course! When do you need it?

**Rachel:**   As soon as possible. Oh, and don't forget to make two photocopies.

**John:**   Did you say make two copies?

**Rachel:**   Yes, two copies.

**John:**   I'll do it right away.

> **Grammar note**
>
> **Polite requests with *could***
> Use *could* to make polite requests.
>   Could you file these letters, please?
>   Could you make two copies, please?

**C** Listen again and repeat.

**D** Work with a partner. Practice the conversation. Use the work tasks in 1A and your own ideas.

**E** Listen to 3 conversations. Write each person's task under the pictures.

| make copies   write an email   send a letter |
| --- |

Jung-ju

Ruth

Simon

1. _____

2. _____

3. _____

## 2 Practice your pronunciation

  **A** **Listen to the 2 recordings of the conversation. When does Simon sound more helpful—in 1 or in 2? Check (✔) your answer.**

**Ruth:** Could you help me with my computer, please?

**Simon:** I'm busy now, but I'll help you later. OK?

☐ Recording 1  ☐ Recording 2

**Need help?**

Intonation can show how a person feels.

Is she upset?
Does he want to help?

**B** **Listen to the conversations. Then practice with a partner.**

1. **A:** Could you make some photocopies, please?
   **B:** Yes, of course.

2. **A:** Could you type these letters, please?
   **B:** Sure! No problem. I can type them this afternoon.

## 3 Real-life math

**A** **Read about Mr. Jones. Answer the questions.**

Mr. Jones is looking for an office assistant. The assistant needs to type very fast. Two people are applying for the job. Sheri can type 210 words in 3 minutes. Joe can type 100 words in 2 minutes.

1. How many words can each person type per minute?
2. Who should Mr. Jones hire, Sheri or Joe?

Sheri

Joe

**B** **How did you solve the problem? Tell a partner.**

**TEST YOURSELF** ✓

Role-play giving and receiving instructions. Partner A: Ask your partner to do a task. Partner B: Respond. Be helpful and clarify the instructions. Then change roles.

## 1 Get ready to read

**A** **Read the definitions.**

attitude: your opinions and feelings about something
complain: say that you are unhappy with something
cooperate: work well with other people
positive: not negative; cheerful

**B** **What do you think? Which words are part of a positive attitude at work? Circle them.**

| | | | | | |
|---|---|---|---|---|---|
| happy | angry | excited | friendly | worried | bored |

## 2 Read about job performance skills

**A** **Read the article.**

# A Positive Attitude

When you start a new job, it's important to show that you have a positive attitude.

*Show that you want to learn.* Read and listen to instructions carefully. Be sure you know the rules of the company, and be sure you understand. Ask questions. It's OK to make mistakes, but you should show that you want to improve.[1] Ask your manager for new tasks.

*Show that you can cooperate.*

Be on time. Call when you are going to be late. Don't just complain about problems. Look for solutions. Look for ways to help co-workers. Answer questions and speak to your co-workers in a helpful way.

It's important to do good work, but a positive attitude is also important. A positive attitude can improve your job evaluation,[2] too.

[1] improve: make something better
[2] job evaluation: job report from your manager

 **B** **Listen and read the article again.**

**C** Choose the correct words. Circle *a* or *b*.

1. You don't understand the instructions.

   You should ____.

   a. make mistakes

   b. ask questions

2. You want to show that you can cooperate.

   You should ____.

   a. read the instructions

   b. help your co-workers

3. You are going to be late.

   You should ____.

   a. call your manager

   b. stay home

4. You are speaking to a co-worker.

   You should sound ____.

   a. helpful

   b. negative

**D** Complete the sentences. Use the words in the box.

| attitude | improve | cooperate | complain |

1. When you work with other people, it's important to _____.
2. Some employees_____ a lot about problems. This shows a negative attitude.
3. He has a positive _____. This will help his job evaluation.
4. A good employee tries to _____ his or her job evaluation every year.

# 3 Read a job evaluation

**A** Read Rosa's job evaluation. What are the problems in her evaluation?

| Employee name: *Rosa Pereira* | COMMENTS: |
|---|---|
| Follows instructions: | *She asks good questions.* |
| Helps others: | *She explains instructions to her co-workers.* |
| Uses time: | *Sometimes she talks too much and doesn't finish her work.* |
| Solves problems: | *She made a new sign with instructions for the fax machine.* |
| Shows a positive attitude: | *She is polite and friendly. She talks to customers.* |
| Is on time for work: | *She was late for work three times in March.* |

Evaluation score: **Excellent** **Good** **Fair**     Signature: *Max Rossi (Manager)*

**B** Think about the questions. Talk about the answers with your class.

1. What's your opinion? How should the manager evaluate Rosa? *Excellent, Good,* or *Fair*?
2. Are job evaluations a good idea? Should employees evaluate their managers, too?

**BRING IT TO LIFE**

Look on the Internet or in the library for 3 different jobs. Find information on hourly pay, the dress code, or safety rules for each job. Tell the class about them.

# 1 Grammar

**A** **Complete the sentences. Use *might (not)* and the words in the box.**

| ~~get a raise~~ | help | get hired | get fired |

**Need help?**

**Expressions with *get***

Many work expressions use the word *get*.

get fired = lose your job
get hired = get a job
get a raise = earn more money

1. I finish my work and have a positive attitude.

   I ____might get a raise____ next year.

2. Tell your co-worker about the problem.

   He _____ you.

3. I was late for the job interview.

   I _____.

4. Don't come to work late very often.

   You _____.

**B** **Complete the sentences with *should (not)* or *might (not)*.**

1. You look cold. You _____should_____ put on a sweater.

2. I'm very cold. I _____ be able to work much longer today.

3. You know, the heater _____ be broken again.

4. We _____ call the manager to tell her.

5. She's in a meeting, so we _____ call her now. Let's call a repair person.

**C** **Write polite requests with *could*. Use the words in parentheses.**

1. (help me use the scanner)

   _Could you help me use the scanner, please?_

2. (type this letter for me)

   _____

3. (call me at 3 o'clock)

   _____

**D** **Complete the sentences with *to* or *X*. (*X* = *to* is not necessary)**

1. All employees should __X__ read their pay stubs carefully.

2. You need ____ understand the deductions.

3. I want ____ learn about gross pay and net pay.

4. The hourly rate for that job might ____ go up next year.

## 2 Group work

**A** Work with 2–3 classmates. Write a conversation with 6–8 lines between the people in the picture. Share your conversations with the class.

A: *Jen, could you help me, please?*
B: *Sure, what is it?*
A: *…*

**B** Interview 3 classmates. Ask: *What do you think you might do in these situations?* Write their answers in your notebook.

Situation 1: You need to use a fax machine. You don't understand the instructions.
Situation 2: You get your pay stub. You don't understand all the deductions.

**C** Talk about the answers with your class.

### PROBLEM SOLVING

**A** Listen and read about Jamal's problem.

Jamal started his job two weeks ago. He works as a ticket collector in the movie theater. He is on time every day. He wears neat clothes. He checks the tickets carefully. But he cannot always understand what the manager says. He is also very shy. He doesn't like to ask, "Could you repeat those instructions, please?" Sometimes he makes mistakes.

**B** Work with your classmates. Answer the questions.

1. What is Jamal's problem?
2. What should he do? Think of 2 or 3 solutions to his problem.

# UNIT 6

## Pick up the Phone

**FOCUS ON**
- phone bills and phone calls
- calling in sick
- the past continuous
- phone messages
- community services

---

**LESSON 1** **Vocabulary**

## 1 Learn to read a phone bill

**A** Look at the phone bill. Name 2 things you learn about Walter.

 **B** Listen and look at the phone bill.

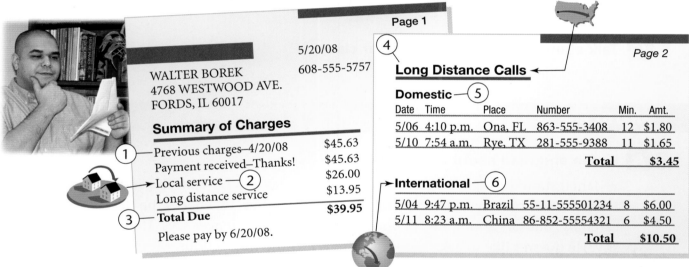

Page 1

5/20/08
608-555-5757

WALTER BOREK
4768 WESTWOOD AVE.
FORDS, IL 60017

### Summary of Charges

| | |
|---|---|
| ① —Previous charges–4/20/08 | $45.63 |
| Payment received–Thanks! | $45.63 |
| —Local service ② | $26.00 |
| Long distance service | $13.95 |
| ③ — **Total Due** | **$39.95** |

Please pay by 6/20/08.

④ **Long Distance Calls**

Page 2

**Domestic** ⑤

| Date | Time | Place | Number | Min. | Amt. |
|---|---|---|---|---|---|
| 5/06 | 4:10 p.m. | Ona, FL | 863-555-3408 | 12 | $1.80 |
| 5/10 | 7:54 a.m. | Rye, TX | 281-555-9388 | 11 | $1.65 |
| | | | **Total** | | **$3.45** |

**International** ⑥

| Date | Time | Place | Number | Min. | Amt. |
|---|---|---|---|---|---|
| 5/04 | 9:47 p.m. | Brazil | 55-11-555501234 | 8 | $6.00 |
| 5/11 | 8:23 a.m. | China | 86-852-55554321 | 6 | $4.50 |
| | | | **Total** | | **$10.50** |

 **C** Listen and repeat the words.

1. previous charges
2. local service
3. total due
4. long distance calls
5. domestic
6. international

**D** Complete the sentences. Read the sentences to a partner.

1. Walter made four __long distance calls__ this month.
2. He made two _____ calls—one to Florida and one to Texas.
3. He made two _____ calls—one to Brazil and one to China.
4. Walter pays $26 for his _____.
5. The _____ on Walter's phone bill were $45.63.
6. The _____ on his bill is $39.95.

---

☑ Interpret a telephone bill; identify types of calls

## 2 Talk about phones and phone calls

**A** **Work with your classmates. Match the words with the pictures.**

_____ answering machine        _____ pay phone                    _____ call a taxi

_____ cell phone               _____ call directory assistance    _____ listen to a message

_1_ cordless phone             _____ call emergency services

**B** **Listen and check your answers. Then practice the words with a partner.**

**C** **Work with a partner. Ask and answer questions. Use the pictures in 2A.**

A: What's Carla doing?

B: She's calling a taxi.

A: What is she using?

B: She's using a pay phone.

**D** **Interview a partner. Ask and answer the questions.**

1. What kinds of phone calls do you usually make?
2. How many calls do you usually make in one week?
3. How many hours do you talk on the phone every week?

---

**TEST YOURSELF** ✔

Close your book. Write 4 words from the phone bill in 1A and 4 kinds of phones or phone calls. Check your spelling in a dictionary.

## 1 Read about calling in sick

**A** Look at the pictures. Match the sentences with the pictures.

_____ Tony, get to work right now!

_____ Hi, Tony! Did you oversleep again?

_1_ Oh, no! I think I'll call in sick today.

_____ Why does this always happen to me?

 **B** Listen and read the story.

**Never Late Again!**

Our manager at the Electronics Hut understands that people can't come to work when they're sick. He also knows that a parent might have to stay home with a sick child. But some employees are absent a lot, and that's a problem.

That was Tony's problem. Tony often got up late. His alarm clock didn't work. Every time he overslept, he called in sick. Then one day last month, the phone rang at 10:30. I answered it, but I didn't see our manager. He was standing near me. "Hi, Tony!" I said. "Did you oversleep again?" The manager heard me! He took the phone and shouted, "Tony, get to work right now!"

That was the last time Tony called in sick. He bought a new alarm clock—and kept his job.

**C** Check your understanding. Mark the sentences T (true) or F (false).

_T_ 1. Tony called in sick all the time.

_____ 2. Tony was sick.

_____ 3. Tony's manager was angry.

_____ 4. Tony got fired.

## 2 Write about being absent

**A** **Think about a time when you were absent from school or work. Answer the questions. Write your answers in a paragraph.**

¹ When were you absent from school or work? ² Why were you absent?
³ Who did you call? ⁴ What did the person say?

_____

I was absent from _____

_____

_____

_____

_____

**Need help?**

A: Why were you absent?
B: I...
   was tired.
   had a toothache.
   missed the bus.
   had a cold.

**B** **Read your paragraph to a partner. Why was your partner absent from school or work?**

## 3 Talk about excuses

**A** **Listen to the phone calls. Number the excuses in the order you hear them.**

_____ My son is sick.      _____ I missed the bus this morning.

_____ I need to help my friend move.      _____ I have a bad cold.

_1_ I have a fever. I feel terrible.      _____ I'm just a little tired today.

**B** **Talk with a partner. Which excuses are appropriate for work? Which excuses are not appropriate?**

**C** **Listen. Then practice the conversation with a partner. Use your own ideas.**

A: I can't come to work today.

B: Why not? What's the matter?

A: My daughter is sick.

B: OK. We'll see you tomorrow then.

A: Thank you. Goodbye.

**TEST YOURSELF** ✔

Close your book. Write 3 excuses that are appropriate for your job or school. Write 3 excuses that are not appropriate. Tell a partner.

## 1 Learn the past continuous

**A** Look at the pictures. Gloria phoned 3 friends yesterday between 8:00 and 8:30 a.m. Who was at home?

① Tania was jogging.

② Stan and Rita were eating breakfast.

③ Filipo was cleaning the house.

**B** Study the charts. Complete the sentences below.

### THE PAST CONTINUOUS

| Affirmative statements | | | | | | |
|---|---|---|---|---|---|---|
| I | was | jogging. | We | | were | jogging. |
| You | were | | You | | | |
| He<br>She | was | | They | | | |

1. I _____ jogging.  2. They were _____.

| Negative statements | | | | | | |
|---|---|---|---|---|---|---|
| I | was not | jogging. | We | | were not | jogging. |
| You | were not | | You | | | |
| He<br>She | was not | | They | | | |

| Contractions |
|---|
| was not = wasn't<br>were not = weren't |

3. He was not _____.  4. We _____ jogging.

**C** What were these people doing this morning? Look at the chart. Then complete the sentences. Use the past continuous.

1. Filipo _was doing the laundry_ at 9:00.
2. Stan and Rita _____ at 11:00.
3. At 11:00, Filipo _____.
4. At 1:00, Stan and Rita _____.

| | Stan and Rita | Filipo |
|---|---|---|
| **9 a.m.** | drive to work | do the laundry |
| **11 a.m.** | work | make lunch |
| **1 p.m.** | eat lunch | go to school |

## 2 Ask and answer questions in the past continuous

**A** Study the charts. Match the questions with the answers below.

| Information questions and answers |
|---|
| **A:** What was Filipo doing at 9 a.m.? <br> **B:** He was doing the laundry. |
| **A:** What were Stan and Rita doing at 9 a.m.? <br> **B:** They were driving to work. |

| Yes/No questions and short answers |
|---|
| **A:** Were you sleeping at 8 a.m.? <br> **B:** No, I wasn't. |
| **A:** Was Rita eating breakfast at 8 a.m.? <br> **B:** Yes, she was. |

_e_ 1. Was Filipo jogging at 9 a.m.?

____ 2. Were Stan and Rita driving at 9 a.m.?

____ 3. What was Filipo doing at 11 a.m.?

____ 4. What were Stan and Rita doing at 1 p.m.?

____ 5. Was Filipo going to school at 1 p.m.?

a. Yes, he was.

b. They were eating lunch.

c. Yes, they were.

d. He was making lunch.

e. No, he wasn't.

**B** Look at the chart in 1C. Write questions for these answers.

1. **A:** <u>What was Filipo doing at 9 a.m.?</u>
   **B:** He was doing the laundry.

2. **A:** _____
   **B:** They were working.

3. **A:** _____
   **B:** No, he wasn't. He was going to school.

4. **A:** _____
   **B:** No, they weren't. They were driving.

## 3 Practice using the past continuous

**A** What were you doing yesterday at each of the times below?
Write your answers in your notebook.

*I was sleeping at 6 a.m.*

**B** Interview a partner. Ask and answer questions about the times.

**A:** *What were you doing at 6 a.m.?*
**B:** *I was sleeping.*

**C** Talk about the answers with your class.

> **TEST YOURSELF** ✓
>
> Write 4 sentences about your schedule yesterday and 4 sentences about
> your partner's schedule yesterday. Use the information in 3A and 3B.

## 1 Learn how to leave and take messages

**A** Read the telephone message. Answer the questions.

1. Who is the message from?
2. Who is the message for?
3. Is Rita late or out sick? Why?

☎ **IMPORTANT MESSAGE**

from    *Rita Gonzalez*

for     *Ms. Mendoza*

message   *Rita is out sick today.*

          *She has a bad cold.*

**B** Listen and read.

**Ana:** Hello. Sam's Supermarket. How can I help you?

**Frank:** Good morning. Can I speak to Ms. Andrews, please?

**Ana:** I'm sorry. She's not in yet. May I take a message?

**Frank:** Yes, please. This is Frank Ramos. I'm a cashier. I'm calling in sick today.

**Ana:** OK. I'll give Ms. Andrews your message.

**Frank:** Thanks a lot! Goodbye.

**C** Listen again and repeat.

**D** Work with a partner. Practice the conversation. Use your own information.

> **Need help?**
>
> **Polite requests**
> Can I speak to…?
> May I speak to…?
> Is…there, please?

**E** Listen to the phone calls. Who is late? Who is out sick? Circle the correct words.

① ☎ MESSAGE

from   Jack Brown

for    Mr. Reed

Jack is (late)/out sick today.

reason

② ☎ MESSAGE

from   Hal Freeman

for    Manager

Hal is late/out sick today.

reason

③ ☎ MESSAGE

from   Maria Ruiz

for    Mr. Green

Maria is late/out sick today.

reason

**F** Listen again. Complete the messages with the reasons below.

(He/She) has a cold.      (He/She) has car problems.      (He/She) has a backache.

## 2 Practice your pronunciation

**A** **Listen to the pronunciation of the words.**

live—I live in California.
leave—I leave work at 5:00.

**B** **Listen. Circle the words you hear.**

1. live    leave    3. fill    feel
2. his    he's    4. will    we'll

**C** **Listen and repeat.**

1. I don't feel well.
2. He's calling in sick.
3. Can I leave a message?
4. I will pay my phone bill.

**D** **Work with a partner. Read the sentences to a partner.**

## 3 Real-life math

**A** **Look at the phone cards. Answer the questions.**

1. How many PhoneSaver cards do you need to get 1,000 minutes? _____
2. Which phone card is a better buy, Dial-a-Phone or PhoneSaver? _____

**PhoneSaver**

250 minutes for $3

**DIAL·A·PHONE**

1,000 minutes for $10

**B** **How did you find the answers? Tell a partner.**

---

**TEST YOURSELF** ✔

Role-play a phone conversation with a partner. Partner A: Call in sick to your school or work. Give a reason. Partner B: Take a message. Then change roles.

## 1 Get ready to read

**A** Read the definitions.

counselor: someone who gives you advice
senior: an older person, often a retired person
senior center: a place where seniors meet,
 take classes, and get advice
volunteer: someone who works without pay

Seniors at a senior center event

**B** Look at the article in 2A. Answer the questions.

1. What four places in the community are mentioned?
2. What do you think people do at these places?

## 2 Read about community services

**A** Read the article.

### Getting and Giving Help in the Community

There are many places in the community where people can get and give help. These services are usually listed in the Community Services section of the telephone directory. Here are just a few services.

**JOB CENTERS:**

At job centers, job counselors help people choose jobs. They also help with applications and interviews. There is a job bank to help people find jobs.

**PUBLIC LIBRARIES:**

Public libraries offer[1] many services for people of all ages. Parents can take their children to the storytelling hour in the children's section. There are book clubs for reading and discussion. There is often free Internet, too.

**SENIOR CENTERS:**

Senior centers offer different kinds of services, information, and advice to men and women over 55. Seniors can enjoy social events,[2] such as parties and movies, and meet other seniors.

**VOLUNTEER CENTERS:**

Volunteer centers have volunteers of all ages helping in hospitals, schools, and senior centers. If you have some free time, you can call a volunteer center and find out how to help others in your community.

[1] offer: give
[2] social event: a time to meet and be with people

**B** Listen and read the article again.

☑ Identify community services; use the telephone directory

**C** Where can you go in these situations? Write the names of the places.

1. I want to find a part-time job. _____a job center_____
2. I want to help children in a hospital. _____
3. My grandmother wants to make some friends. _____
4. My daughter loves to listen to stories. _____

**D** Complete the sentences. Use the words in the box.

| offer | counselor | volunteer | social | ~~senior~~ |
|-------|-----------|-----------|--------|-----------|

1. A place where older people can meet is a _____senior_____ center.
2. A job _____ helps people choose jobs.
3. A _____ works without pay.
4. You can meet people at a _____ event.
5. Public libraries _____ free Internet services.

# 3 Read a phone directory

**A** Look at the phone directory. What services should these people call? Write the phone numbers.

1. Dave asks, "When does the library open on Sundays?" _____
2. Paula asks, "How can I volunteer at the Senior Center?" _____
3. Yoshi asks, "Where can I take English classes?"

   _____

**Social & Human Services**

**Education Services**
Adult Education Services . . . . . . .555-6700
Health Education Center . . . . . . .555-2167
Public Library . . . . . . . . . . . . . .555-4121

**Employment Services**
Career Counseling . . . . . . . . . . .555-8890
Job Center . . . . . . . . . . . . . . . .555-8069

**Volunteer Services**
Senior Volunteer Center . . . . . . .555-8977
Literacy Volunteers . . . . . . . . . . .555-8906

**B** Think about the questions. Talk about the answers with your class.

1. Where is your local library? Do you like to go to the library?
2. Where is the senior center in your community? Do you know seniors who go to a senior center?

**BRING IT TO LIFE**

Find the names, addresses, and phone numbers of 3 community services in the telephone directory or on the Internet. Make a list of the services with your classmates.

## 1 Grammar

**A** Write the *-ing* forms of the verbs in the chart.

| Verbs | *-ing* form | Verbs | *-ing* form |
|-------|-------------|-------|-------------|
| drive | driving | open | |
| write | | take | |
| read | | wait | |
| eat | | sleep | |

**Grammar note**

**Verbs with *-ing***

For words that end in *-e*, change the *-e* to *-ing*.

drive → driving

**B** Circle the correct words.

1. I didn't ( (go) / going ) to work yesterday.
2. I wasn't ( work / working ) at 7:00 last night.
3. What were you ( do / doing ) yesterday at 4:30 in the afternoon?
4. Did Joe ( call / calling ) in sick last Monday?
5. Were they ( talk / talking ) on the phone at 2 a.m.?

**C** Read the information in the chart. Write questions and answers.

| | **Nuria** | **Rick and Colette** |
|-------|-----------|----------------------|
| **5 p.m.** | drive home | wait for a train |
| **6 p.m.** | make dinner | shop for food |
| **7 p.m.** | watch TV | make dinner |

INFORMATION QUESTIONS

1. Nuria / 5 p.m.

   What was Nuria doing at 5 p.m. ?

   She was driving home          .

2. Rick and Colette / 6 p.m.

   _____ ?

   _____ .

3. Nuria / 7 p.m.

   _____ ?

   _____ .

YES/NO QUESTIONS

4. Rick and Colette / make dinner / 7 p.m.

   Were Rick and Colette making dinner at 7 p.m. ?

   Yes, _____ .

5. Nuria / drive home / 6 p.m.

   _____ ?

   _____ .

6. Rick and Colette / watch TV / 7 p.m.

   _____ ?

   _____ .

# 2 Group work

**A** Work with 2–3 classmates. Write a conversation with 6–8 lines between the people in the picture. Share your conversation with the class.

**A:** *Good morning. Could I speak to Mr. Robertson, please?*

**B:** *He's not in. Can I take a message?*

**A:** *Yes,…*

**B** Interview 3 classmates. Write their answers in the chart.

1. When was the last time you left a phone message?
2. Who was it for?
3. What was it about?

| | Phone messages | | |
| --- | --- | --- | --- |
| Classmates' names | When...? | Who...for? | What...? |
| 1. | | | |
| 2. | | | |
| 3. | | | |

**C** Talk about the answers with your class.

## PROBLEM SOLVING

**A** Listen and read about Janet's problem.

  Janet's son, Timmy, is three years old. She takes him to a childcare center every morning at 7:00. Then she goes to work. Timmy often gets sick. Last winter he had colds four different times. Timmy is sick again today, and he can't go to the childcare center. Janet can't stay home with him. She has to go to work. She has no more sick days this year.

**B** Work with your classmates. Answer the questions.

1. What is Janet's problem?
2. What can she do? Think of 2 or 3 solutions to her problem.

# UNIT 7

# What's for Dinner?

**FOCUS ON**
- weights and measurements
- shopping and food prices
- count and noncount nouns
- locating things at the supermarket
- nutrition and health

## LESSON 1 Vocabulary

## 1 Learn container words

**A** Look at the pictures. Name the food you see.

**B** Listen and look at the pictures.

**C** Listen and repeat the words.

| | | | |
|---|---|---|---|
| 1. box | 3. can | 5. package | 7. bag |
| 2. jar | 4. carton | 6. bottle | 8. bunch |

**D** Complete the sentences. Read the sentences to a partner.

1. A ___carton___ of milk is $1.29.
2. A _____ of oil is $5.99.
3. A _____ of peanut butter is $2.69.
4. A _____ of potato chips is $1.99.
5. A _____ of bananas is $1.59.
6. A _____ of soup is $0.99.
7. A _____ of spaghetti is $0.79.
8. A _____ of cookies is $2.59.

☑ Identify product containers; interpret weights and measurements

## 2 Talk about weights and measurements

**A** **Work with your classmates. Match the words with the picture.**

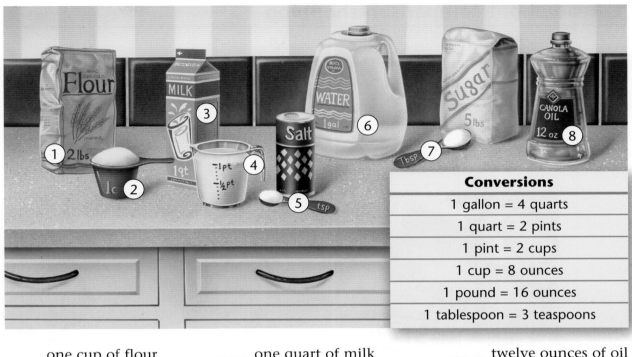

**Conversions**

| |
| --- |
| 1 gallon = 4 quarts |
| 1 quart = 2 pints |
| 1 pint = 2 cups |
| 1 cup = 8 ounces |
| 1 pound = 16 ounces |
| 1 tablespoon = 3 teaspoons |

____ one cup of flour     ____ one quart of milk     ____ twelve ounces of oil

____ one gallon of water     ____ one tablespoon of sugar     _1_ two pounds of flour

____ one pint of milk     ____ one teaspoon of salt

**B** **Listen and check your answers. Then practice the words with a partner.**

**C** **Complete the sentences. Use the chart in 2A.**

1. There are 16 ____ounces____ in 1 pound of flour.

2. There are 2 _____ in 1 quart of milk.

3. There are 4 quarts in 1 _____ of water.

4. There are 3 _____ in 1 tablespoon of sugar.

5. There are 8 _____ in 1 cup of milk.

**D** **Interview a partner. Ask questions using container and measurement words.**

*How many boxes of cereal do you buy in one week?*

*How many pounds of sugar do you buy in one month?*

**TEST YOURSELF** ✓

Close your book. Write 5 container words and 5 measurement words.
Check your spelling in a dictionary.

# 1 Read about comparison shopping

**A** Look at the pictures and the title of the story in 1B. Guess the answers to the questions. Circle *a* or *b*.

1. This story is about saving money _____.
   a. at the mall
   b. at the supermarket

2. This story talks about _____.
   a. coupons
   b. credit cards

supermarket flyer

coupon

store brand

UNIT PRICE
28¢ per oz.
you pay
$1.68
6 oz.

unit-price label

STUDENT AUDIO

**B** Listen and read the story.

## Save at the Supermarket
by Jung Kim

Jung Kim

It's important for me to save money at the supermarket. I have five children, and they eat a lot! I go to the supermarket every week. Before I go, I read the supermarket advertisements and compare prices in different stores. Then I go to the supermarket with lower prices.

At the supermarket, I check the unit prices. I also buy store brands. They're usually cheaper than name brands. I always use coupons, and I try to save money on food like bread, milk, and fruit. The children always want a lot of chips and cookies, but I tell them, "Fruit is better for you."

**C** Check your understanding. Mark the sentences T (true) or F (false).

___T___ 1. Jung Kim goes to the supermarket every week.

_____ 2. She compares prices in different stores.

_____ 3. She doesn't read the unit prices.

_____ 4. She uses coupons to save money.

## 2 Write about saving money

**A** Write about yourself. Complete the paragraph.

_____

    I usually buy food at _____. How do I save money?
Well, I _____, and I _____. I usually
save money on _____. I sometimes spend too much money
on _____.

**B** Read your paragraph to a partner. How does your partner save money?


## 3 Compare prices

**A** Listen to Mrs. Kim and her friend compare prices. Look at the labels. Which jam does Mrs. Kim buy?

Berry Good
Jam 8 oz.

| 20¢ per oz. | $1.60 8 oz. |

Net wt.   8oz.

Berry Fine
Jam 12 oz.

| 30¢ per oz. | $3.60 12 oz. |

Net wt.   12oz.

**B** Look at the labels. Check (✔) the better buys.

| Dairy Day Milk 1 qt. | Dairy Day Milk 1/2 gal. | HomeMade Soup 10 oz. | Best's Soup 18 oz. |
|---|---|---|---|
| $5.20 per gal.   $1.30 1 qt. | $4.40 per gal.   $2.20 1/2 gal. | 12¢ per oz.   $1.20 10 oz. | 10¢ per oz.   $1.80 18 oz. |

1. ☐ 1 quart of Dairy Day Milk
   ☐ 1/2 gallon of Dairy Day Milk

2. ☐ 10 ounces of HomeMade Soup
   ☐ 18 ounces of Best's Soup

**C** Listen. Then practice the conversation with a partner. Use the labels in 3B.

   **A:** Which milk is a better buy, one quart for $1.30 or half a gallon for $2.20?

   **B:** Look at the unit-price label. Half a gallon for $2.20 is cheaper.

   **A:** Oh, yes. It's only $4.40 per gallon. The other one is $5.20.

---

**TEST YOURSELF** ✔

Close your book. Write 5 ways to save money at the supermarket.
Tell a partner.

## 1 Learn about count and noncount nouns

**A** Read Soledad's favorite recipe. Answer the questions.

1. How many onions does Soledad need?
2. How much cheese does she need?
3. Is there any sugar in the casserole?

**Vegetable Casserole**

●●●●●●●●●●●●●●●●●●●●

| | |
|---|---|
| 3 onions | 2 tbsp. flour |
| 6 potatoes | 8 oz. cheese |
| 3 tbsp. butter | 1/4 c. milk |
| 6 large mushrooms | 1 tsp. salt |
| 4 medium tomatoes | 1/2 tsp. pepper |

First, chop the onions and the potatoes.
Then, melt the butter in a frying pan and →

**B** Study the charts. Add the words in the box to the charts.

| bananas    olive oil    spaghetti    cookies |
|---|

| Count nouns (1 onion, 2 onions) | Noncount nouns (some butter) |
|---|---|
| onions | butter |
| potatoes | flour |
| mushrooms | cheese |
| tomatoes | milk |
| _____ | _____ |
| _____ | _____ |

**C** Study the charts. Complete the sentences below.

| *How many* with count nouns | | | *How much* with noncount nouns | | |
|---|---|---|---|---|---|
| How many | onions tomatoes | do we need? | How much | flour salt | do we need? |

1. How _____ onions do we need?   2. How _____ salt do we need?

**D** Complete the questions. Use *How much* or *How many*.

1. _____ tomatoes do we need?
2. _____ milk do we need?
3. _____ butter do we need?
4. _____ mushrooms do we need?
5. _____ flour do we need?

## 2 Statements with count and noncount nouns

**A** Study the chart. Complete the sentences below. Circle *a* or *b*.

|  | Affirmative statements | Negative statements |
|---|---|---|
| **Count nouns** | We need an onion.<br>We need two tomatoes. | We don't need a carrot.<br>We don't need (any) potatoes. |
| **Noncount nouns** | We need some cheese.<br>We need one ounce of oil. | We don't need (any) milk. |

1. We need one _____ for the salad.
   a. onion
   b. oil

2. You need two _____ for this recipe.
   a. milk
   b. tomatoes

3. They don't need any _____ for the salad.
   a. cheese
   b. milk

4. There's some _____ in the salad.
   a. oil
   b. potatoes

**B** Complete the sentences. Use *a, an, some,* or *any*.

1. She needs _____ ounce of chocolate.
2. They have _____ potatoes for the soup.
3. Mike has _____ bottle of water.
4. I don't want _____ cheese on my pizza.

chocolate

## 3 Practice questions with *How much* and *How many*

**A** Complete the questions with *How much* or *How many*. Find people with these things in their kitchen. Write their names in the chart.

| Find someone with... | Ask classmates... | Names |
|---|---|---|
| 1. five apples | How many apples do you have in your kitchen? | |
| 2. one carton of milk | _____ milk do you have in your kitchen? | |
| 3. one bottle of oil | _____ oil do you have in your kitchen? | |
| 4. two oranges | _____ oranges do you have in your kitchen? | |

**B** Talk about your information with the class.

*Moy has five apples in his kitchen.*

**TEST YOURSELF** ✔

Write 5 sentences about your classmates. Use the information in the chart in 3A.
*Marsha has one carton of milk in her kitchen.*

## **1** Learn how to ask for the location of items in the supermarket

**A** Where can you find these foods? Write the aisle or section under each food.

grapes _produce_   soup _____

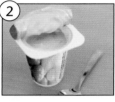

yogurt _____   sausages _____

**B** Listen and read.

Customer: Excuse me. Where's the bread, please?
Clerk: Bread? It's in aisle 1, next to the cookies.
Customer: Thanks. Oh, and the tomatoes?
Clerk: They're in the produce section.
Customer: OK. Thanks a lot.

> **Grammar note**
>
> **Review: verbs**
> Where **are** the eggs?
> Where **is** the bread?

**C** Listen again and repeat.

**D** Work with a partner. Practice the conversation.
Use the information in 1A or your own ideas.

**E** Listen. What are the customers looking for? Circle the correct words.

a. eggs
b. bread
c. butter
_dairy section_

a. soup
b. juice
c. jam
_____

a. fruit
b. sausages
c. chicken
_____

**F** Listen again. Write the aisle or section.

☑ Ask for and give the location of merchandise

## 2 Practice your pronunciation

**A** **Listen to these words in the singular and plural. How many syllables are there in each word?**

1. egg    eggs      3. box    boxes
2. apple   apples    4. package   packages

> **Need help?**
>
> Some words end in sounds like *s* (as in *box* or *dress*), *ge* (as in *page*), or *ch* (as in *lunch*).
> For these words, add an extra syllable in the plural.
>
> box → boxes     page → pages
> dress → dresses   lunch → lunches

**B** **Which plurals have an extra syllable? Write the words in the chart. Then listen and check your answers.**

| No extra syllable | Extra syllable |
|---|---|
| grapes | |
| | |
| | |
| | |

| | |
|---|---|
| ~~grapes~~ | oranges |
| sausages | lunches |
| jars | bunches |
| mushrooms | cartons |

**C** **Read the sentences to a partner.**

1. I need some grapes.
2. They have two jars of jam.
3. He wants some oranges.
4. Give me two bunches of bananas, please.

## 3 Real-life math

**A** **Mr. Wu went to Roy's Market. He had 2 coupons, and there was a 2 for 1 sale on bread. Read the receipt and answer the questions.**

1. How much did Mr. Wu save?

   _____

2. How much did he pay?

   _____

**B** **How did you find the answers? Tell a partner.**

**Roy's Market**

| | | |
|---|---|---|
| Rice | 2.23 | |
| | -1.00 | (coupon) |
| Butter | 2.79 | |
| | -0.50 | (coupon) |
| Jam | 2.39 | |
| Bread | 2.30 | |
| Bread | 2.30 | |
| | -2.30 | (sale) |
| Bananas | 1.45 | |

**Total (before savings)**
      **$13.46**

*Savings* - _____

You pay _____

---

**TEST YOURSELF** ✔

Role-play a conversation in a supermarket. Partner A: Ask for the location of an item in the supermarket. Partner B: Answer the question. Then change roles.

## 1 Get ready to read

**A**  **Read the definitions.**

calcium: something in food that makes bones and teeth strong
calories: the amount of energy in a food
diet: the food a person eats
lean meat: meat that has very little fat

**B**  **How often do you eat these foods? Write the numbers below.**

| 0 = never | 2 = twice a week | 4 = four times a week |
|---|---|---|
| 1 = once a week | 3 = three times a week | 5 = every day |

_____ fruit          _____ rice          _____ bread

_____ chocolate          _____ milk          _____ vegetables

## 2 Read about food and health

**A**  **Read the article.**

# Good Food for Good Health

For a healthy lifestyle, it is important to eat the right foods and stay active. The USDA[1] booklet _Dietary Guidelines for Americans_ gives information and advice. A plan based on about 2,000 calories a day includes:

- about two cups of fruit and two cups of vegetables, especially dark green and orange ones.
- about three ounces of whole-grain[2] bread, rice, or pasta.

- three cups of food with a lot of calcium, for example, low-fat or fat-free milk, yogurt, or cheese.
- lean meat, chicken, fish, eggs, beans, or nuts.
- very small amounts of food with fat, salt, or sugar.

Exercise is also important. Most adults should be physically active for at least 30 minutes every day. Children and teenagers need at least 60 minutes of physical activity. With the right diet and the right amount of exercise, you will feel better today and be healthier in the future.

[1] USDA: United States Department of Agriculture
[2] whole-grain: brown bread and brown rice are examples of whole-grain foods

STUDENT
AUDIO

**B**  **Listen and read the article again.**

**C** Mark the sentences T (true) or F (false).

_T_ 1. The dietary guidelines help people choose food for a healthy diet.

____ 2. You should eat fruit and vegetables every day.

____ 3. You should eat food with a lot of salt and sugar.

____ 4. Children and teenagers don't need to exercise.

**D** Complete the sentences. Use the words in the box.

| lean    calories    calcium    whole-grain |

1. Milk, yogurt, and cheese contain _____.

2. You should eat more _____ bread than white bread.

3. You can eat _____ meat and fish as part of a healthy diet.

4. Some people eat 2,000 _____ a day.

## 3 Read a nutrition label

**A** Read the nutrition label. Answer the questions.

1. How much is one serving?

_____ *1 cup* _____

2. How many servings are in one container?

_____

3. How many calories are there in one serving?

_____

4. How many ingredients are in this soup?

_____

**NUTRITION FACTS**

SERVING* SIZE: **1 CUP**
SERVINGS PER CONTAINER
ABOUT **3**

CALORIES PER SERVING
**120**

INGREDIENTS:
black beans, celery,
spinach, onion, oil,
tomato paste, salt

*serving: amount of food that
a person eats at one time

**B** Think about the questions. Talk about the answers with the class.

1. Why should you read nutrition labels?
2. What healthy foods are in your diet now? Which foods
   do you want to add?

**BRING IT TO LIFE**

Look for a nutrition label on a food product at home or at the supermarket. Bring
the product to class. Tell the class about the information on the label.

# 1 Grammar

**A** Which expression do you use with the words in the chart?
Check (✔) *How much* or *How many*.

|          | How much...? | How many...? |
|----------|:---:|:---:|
| sugar    | ✔   |     |
| cheese   |     |     |
| onions   |     |     |
| mushrooms |    |     |
| milk     |     |     |

**B** Circle the correct words.

1. There ( is / are ) a lot of water in the glass.
2. There ( is / are ) three oranges in the refrigerator.
3. There ( is / are ) too much cheese on the pizza.
4. There ( is / are ) a green pepper in the salad.
5. There ( is / are ) a pound of mushrooms in the casserole.
6. There ( is / are ) two tablespoons of sugar in the cake.

> **Grammar note**
>
> **Review: *There is/There are***
>
> There is one tomato.
> There is some milk.
> There are four cups.

**C** Unscramble the questions.

1. coffee / how much / drink / you / every day / do
   <u>How much coffee do you drink every day?</u>

2. in a week / do / eat / they / How many / oranges

   _____

3. of milk / cartons / have / at home / do / we / How many

   _____

4. salt / How much / use / does / in his meals / he

   _____

**D** Complete the sentences. Use *a*, *an*, *some*, or *any*.

1. I'd like _____<u>some</u>_____ mushrooms on my pizza.
2. Do you want _____ banana?
3. Can I have _____ apple, please?
4. Do you want _____ cup of tea?
5. I don't want _____ milk.
6. There's _____ flour in this bag.

# 2 Group work

**A** Work with 2–3 classmates. Write 2 conversations of 4–6 lines between the people in the picture. Share your conversations with the class.

A: *Excuse me. Where is the bread, please?*
B: *The bread is in aisle 4, next to...*

**B** Interview 3 classmates. Write their answers in the chart.

ASK:
How much/How many _____ do you eat every week?
How much/How many _____ do you drink every week?

| Classmates' names | 1. | 2. | 3. |
|---|---|---|---|
| coffee | | | |
| water | | | |
| cookies | | | |
| bananas | | | |
| rice | | | |

**C** Talk about the answers with your class.

## PROBLEM SOLVING

**A** Listen and read about Dee's problem.

   I work late every day, and I don't have much time to cook. At work, I eat too many snacks and too much sugar. Chocolate and potato chips are my favorite snacks. After work, I am too tired to cook. I prepare quick foods, like a can of soup. These foods have too much salt and sugar. I know this isn't good for me, but I'm very busy.

**B** Work with your classmates. Answer the questions.

1. What is Dee's problem?
2. What can she do? Think of 2 or 3 solutions to her problem.

# Stay Safe and Well

**FOCUS ON**
- illnesses and symptoms
- accessing health-care services
- the past continuous and simple past
- medical prescriptions
- first aid and accident reports

## LESSON **1**  Vocabulary

### **1** Learn about medications

 **A** Look at the pictures. Name the parts of the body you see.

 **B** Listen and look at the pictures.

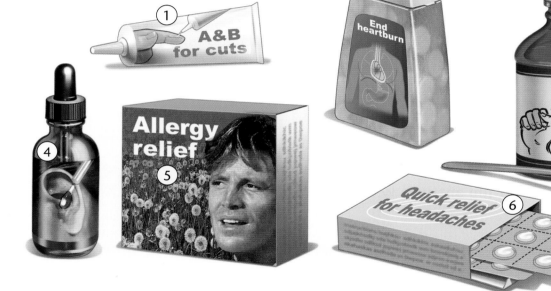

**C** Listen and repeat the words.

| | | |
|---|---|---|
| 1. antibiotic ointment | 3. cough syrup | 5. antihistamine |
| 2. antacid | 4. eardrops | 6. pain reliever |

**D** Complete the sentences. Read the sentences to a partner.

1. The _____eardrops_____ are for an earache.
2. The _____ is for a cough.
3. The _____ is for a headache.
4. The _____ is for a cut finger.
5. The _____ is for heartburn.
6. The _____ is for an allergy.

✔ Identify medications; describe symptoms of illnesses

## 2 Talk about illnesses and symptoms

**A** Work with your classmates. Match the words with the pictures.

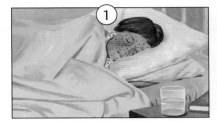

Gina has the measles.

Olivia has the flu.

Ah-choo!

Carlos is allergic to flowers.

Van has a cold.

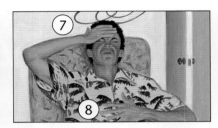

Abdul feels sick to his stomach.

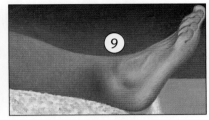

Jiang has a sprained ankle.

| _____ be dizzy | _____ have a cough | __1__ have a rash |
| _____ be nauseous | _____ have a fever | _____ have a runny nose |
| _____ be swollen | _____ have a headache | _____ sneeze |

STUDENT AUDIO

**B** Listen and check your answers. Then practice the words with a partner.

**C** Complete the sentences.

1. I have a headache. I feel hot, too. I think I have a _____ fever _____.

2. I need to _____. Ah-choo! Ah-choo! Maybe I'm allergic to cats.

3. My daughter has a _____ on her face. She might have the measles.

4. Ugh! My stomach! I'm _____ and dizzy. Maybe I ate something bad.

5. Oh, no! I have a _____. Do you have a tissue?

6. My ankle is _____, and it hurts. Do you think it's sprained?

7. Do you have any cough syrup? I have a terrible _____.

**D** Work with a partner. Practice the conversation. Use your own ideas.

A: Hello, Keisha. What's the matter?

B: I have a headache, and I am dizzy.

A: Hmm. Maybe you should call the doctor.

**TEST YOURSELF** ✔

Close your book. Write 5 words for illnesses and 5 words for symptoms. Check your spelling in a dictionary.

## 1 Read about health-care providers

**A** Look at the pictures and the title of the story in 1B. Guess what is happening in each picture.

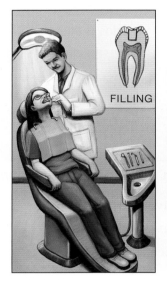   

FILLING

The Heart

Ah-choo!

Dr. Sakara
Pediatrician

**B** Listen and read the story.

### Lina's Terrible Week

Poor Lina! What a terrible week! On Monday, Lina was eating a sandwich when she suddenly got a terrible toothache. She went to the dentist and got a filling in her tooth. On Tuesday, Lina had an appointment with the dental hygienist. The hygienist cleaned her teeth.

On Wednesday morning, Lina's children were both coughing and sneezing. She made an appointment to see the pediatrician. The pediatrician gave the children a prescription for some antibiotics.

On Friday, she had a backache. She went to the chiropractor. He said, "You have to rest for a couple of days."

Poor Lina! Four doctors' visits in five days is too many!

**C** Check your understanding. Mark the sentences T (true) or F (false).

_F_ 1. The dentist cleaned Lina's teeth on Tuesday.

____ 2. The hygienist gave Lina a prescription.

____ 3. Lina went to see the pediatrician about her cough.

____ 4. Lina saw the chiropractor for her backache.

## 2 Write about a medical visit

**A** Write about yourself. Complete the paragraph.

_____

Last _____, I had a _____, and I went to the
    (week/month/year)

_____. The _____ gave me _____.

_____ said, "_____." Now, I feel better.
  (She/He)

**B** Read your paragraph to a partner. What did your partner write about?

## 3 Make an appointment

**A** Listen to the conversations. Write the appointments.

① You have an appointment
   with Dr. Briggs:

   Time _____

   Date _____

② You have an appointment
   with Dr. Richmond:

   Time _____

   Date _____

③ You have an appointment
   with Dr. Garcia:

   Time _____

   Date _____

**B** Listen again. Who will see the chiropractor?

**C** Listen and repeat.

A: Good morning. This is Joe Green. I need to see the doctor.

B: What's the problem?

A: I have a bad cough.

B: How about 3:45 this afternoon?

A: Could you make it after 4:30, please?

B: Yes, of course. How about 4:45?

A: That's good. Thank you.

**D** Work with a partner. Make appointments for these symptoms.

| toothache | backache | fever | sprained ankle | cough |
|---|---|---|---|---|

**TEST YOURSELF** ✔

Close your book. Make a list of health-care providers and the reasons people
visit them. Talk about your ideas with a partner.

## 1 Learn the past continuous and simple past

**A** Look at the pictures. Read the sentences. Then answer the questions.

1. What happened to Carol when she fell?   2. Did Sam hurt his leg?

Carol was skiing when she fell.
She broke her leg.

Sam and Amy were driving when they had an accident.
Sam hurt his back. Amy cut her hand.

**B** Study the charts and the picture. Complete the sentences below.

Carol was skiing            when she broke her leg.

| Past continuous | Simple past | |
|---|---|---|
| Carol was skiing | when | she broke her leg. |
| Sam and Amy were driving | | they had an accident. |

| Present | Past |
|---|---|
| break | broke |
| cut | cut |
| fall | fell |
| hurt | hurt |

1. Carol was skiing when she _____ her leg.
2. Sam and Amy _____ when they had an accident.

**C** Make sentences. Use the past continuous and simple past.

1. Helen / cook / dinner / when / she / burn / her hand
   _Helen was cooking dinner when she burned her hand._

2. Lina / eat / a sandwich / when / she / get / a toothache
   _____

3. I / carry / books / when / I / hurt / my back
   _____

4. Julio and Emil / paint / the house / when / they / fall / off the ladder
   _____

## 2 Ask and answer questions using past forms

**A** Match the questions with the answers.

_____ 1. What happened to Carol's leg?
_____ 2. What was she doing?
_____ 3. What happened to Amy and Sam?
_____ 4. Were they driving to work?

a. They had an accident.
b. She was skiing.
c. Yes, they were.
d. She broke it.

**B** Complete the conversations.

1. **A:** I burned my hand.
   **B:** What ___*were you doing*___?
   **A:** I was cooking.

2. **A:** I broke my tooth when I was eating.
   **B:** Did you go to the dentist?
   **A:** No, _____. I'll go tomorrow.

3. **A:** Steve hurt his finger.
   **B:** What _____?
   **A:** He was riding his bike.

4. **A:** Julio had an accident.
   **B:** _____ working when it happened?
   **A:** Yes, _____.

## 3 Practice using past forms

**A** Work with a partner. Make conversations about the pictures.

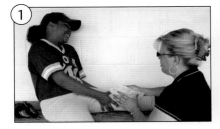

Mariela

1

Alan

2

Trina

3

**A:** Mariela hurt her knee last week.
**B:** What was she doing when it happened?
**A:** She was playing baseball.

**B** Share your conversations with the class.

**Need help?**

**Injuries**
broke her leg
hurt her knee
cut his foot

**TEST YOURSELF** ✔

Write 2 sentences to describe each picture in 3A. Use the simple past and past continuous. Read your sentences to a partner.

## 1 Learn how to ask about prescriptions

**A** Read the prescription label. Answer the questions.

1. What is Mario's problem?
2. Can he take 12 pills in 24 hours?
3. How many times can he refill the prescription?

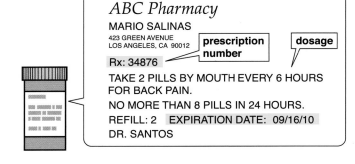

*ABC Pharmacy*
MARIO SALINAS
423 GREEN AVENUE
LOS ANGELES, CA 90012  | prescription number |   | dosage |
Rx: 34876
TAKE 2 PILLS BY MOUTH EVERY 6 HOURS FOR BACK PAIN.
NO MORE THAN 8 PILLS IN 24 HOURS.
REFILL: 2    EXPIRATION DATE: 09/16/10
DR. SANTOS

**B** Listen and read.

| | |
|---|---|
| **Mario:** | Could you refill my prescription, please? |
| **Pharmacist:** | What's your prescription number? |
| **Mario:** | It's 34876. |
| **Pharmacist:** | Is your last name Salinas? |
| **Mario:** | Yes, that's right. My first name is Mario. |
| **Pharmacist:** | OK. Just a moment. |
| **Mario:** | How often should I take the pills? Once a day? |
| **Pharmacist:** | No, you should take two pills every six hours, but only when you are in pain. Don't take more than eight pills a day. |
| **Mario:** | OK. Thanks a lot. |

**Need help?**

**Frequency expressions**
How often...?
   once a day
   twice a day
   three times a day
   every two hours

**C** Listen again and repeat.

**D** Work with a partner. Practice the conversation. Use the prescription in 1A or your own ideas.

**E** Listen to the 3 conversations. Complete the prescription labels.

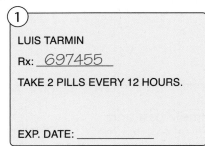

① 
LUIS TARMIN
Rx: _697455_
TAKE 2 PILLS EVERY 12 HOURS.



EXP. DATE: _____

② 
LIN DAWSON
Rx: 895328
TAKE 1 PILL EVERY ____ HOURS.
NO MORE THAN ____ PILLS A DAY.

REFILL: ____ BEFORE 02/28/08

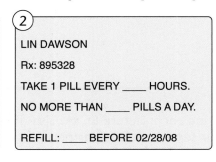

③ 
FATIMA _____
Rx: 692493
TAKE ____ PILL TWICE A DAY, WITH MEALS.

EXP. DATE: 05/20/10

## 2 Ask questions about prescriptions

**A** Study the charts. Complete the questions below with *do* or *does*.

| Information questions with *have to* |
| --- |
| How many pills do I have to take? |
| How often does he have to take these pills? |

| *Yes/No* questions and answers with *have to* | |
| --- | --- |
| **A:** Do I have to take them with food? | **A:** Does she have to stay in bed? |
| **B:** Yes, you do. *or* No, you don't. | **B:** Yes, she does. *or* No, she doesn't. |

1. How many pills _____does_____ he have to take?

2. How often _____ I have to take these pills?

3. _____ she have to take the pills with food?

4. _____ you have to take this medicine with water?

**B** Match the questions with the answers.

__c__ 1. How often do I have to take these pills?          a. Four pills a day.

____ 2. How many pills do I have to take?          b. Yes, you do.

____ 3. How long do I have to take these pills?          c. Once a day.

____ 4. Do I have to take them with meals?          d. For two weeks.

## 3 Real-life math

**A** Read the label. Complete the sentences.

1. You have to take _____ pills a day.

2. This bottle contains _____ pills.

3. You will finish the pills in this bottle in

   _____ days.

> ### ABC Pharmacy
> **LINDA SALINAS**
> 423 GREEN AVENUE
> LOS ANGELES, CA  90012
>
> Rx: 574810
>
> TAKE 2 PILLS BY MOUTH 3 TIMES A DAY.
> NO MORE THAN 6 PILLS EVERY 24 HOURS.
>
> QUANTITY: 60 PILLS
>
> REFILL: 3 BEFORE 11/04/08

**B** How did you find the answers? Tell a partner.

---

**TEST YOURSELF** ✔
Role-play a conversation. Partner A: You are a pharmacist.
Partner B: You are a customer. Ask and answer questions about a prescription.
Then change roles.

## 1 Get ready to read

**A** Read the definitions.

first aid: basic medical treatment in an emergency before a doctor or ambulance arrives

injured: hurt

supplies: things people need for their work or activities

**B** Look at the picture in the article. Which of these supplies is NOT in the first-aid kit?

| bandages | antibiotic ointment | scissors | gloves |

## 2 Read about a first-aid kit

**A** Read the article.

### Preparing a First-Aid Kit

In an emergency, you or someone in your family might be injured. It is important to have a first-aid kit with some basic supplies. You should have one first-aid kit in your home and one in your car. Here are some things you might find in a first-aid kit.

**For small cuts or burns:**
• bandages of different sizes
• antibiotic ointment
• antiseptic wipes (for cleaning cuts)
• scissors (for cutting bandages)

**For someone with a fever or pain:**
• a thermometer (for taking a temperature)
• non-prescription medicines, such as the pain reliever acetaminophen

Where should you put your first-aid kit? It should be in a place that is easy for you to get to but where children cannot find it. It should be in a plastic box, and the box should be easy to open. Check the supplies in your first-aid kit often. Check the expiration dates of medicines.

Remember! In a serious emergency,[1] you should always call emergency services. Ask them how to use first aid before the doctor or other help arrives.

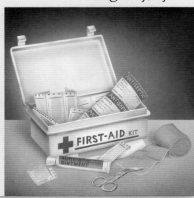

[1] serious emergency: a very bad emergency

  **B** Listen and read the article again.

STUDENT
AUDIO

☑ Interpret simple first-aid procedures; interpret an accident report

**C** Choose the correct words. Circle *a* or *b*.

1. Antibiotic ointment is good for ____.
   - a. small cuts
   - b. a fever
2. You can use antiseptic wipes to ____.
   - a. clean cuts
   - b. cut bandages
3. Acetaminophen is a ____ medicine.
   - a. prescription
   - b. non-prescription
4. You use first aid ____ an ambulance arrives.
   - a. before
   - b. after

**D** Complete the sentences. Use the words in the box.

| scissors | serious | thermometer | expiration |
|----------|---------|-------------|------------|

1. You can take your temperature with a _____.
2. You can use _____ for cutting bandages.
3. Don't use this medicine. The _____ date was October 23rd.
4. In a _____ emergency, you should call emergency services.

# 3 Read an accident report

**A** Read the accident report. Answer the questions.

1. Who is the report about?
   Mario Salinas
2. Where did the accident happen?
   _____
3. When did it happen?
   _____
4. When did Mario report the accident?
   _____

**Accident Report**

Date and time of accident: 9/25/07 at 6:00 p.m.
Place of accident: delivery area
Name: Mario Salinas
Address: 423 Green Avenue,
Los Angeles, CA 90012
Occupation: truck driver
Description of injury: I was lifting some heavy
boxes when I hurt my back.
Date and time of report: 9/25/07 at 7:30 p.m.
Signed by: Mario Salinas

**B** Think about the questions. Talk about the answers with your class.

1. Why do you have to report accidents at work?
2. What are some common accidents in the workplace?
3. What kinds of first-aid supplies do people use at work or school?

**BRING IT TO LIFE**

Find information about first-aid kits on the Internet or at a pharmacy. How much do the kits cost? What's in them? Talk about your information with the class.

## 1 Grammar

**A** **Write the simple past forms of the verbs in the chart.**

| Verbs | Simple past | Verbs | Simple past |
|-------|-------------|-------|-------------|
| start |             | hurt  |             |
| break |             | fall  |             |
| cut   |             | burn  |             |
| drive |             | get   |             |

**B** **Write sentences. Use the past continuous and simple past.**

1. Nina / make / hamburgers / when / she / burn / her finger

   _Nina was making hamburgers when she burned her finger._

2. Michael / fix / window / when / he / hurt / his arm

   _____

3. Amy and Sam / go / home / when / they / have / an accident

   _____

4. Fatima / walk / to work / when / she / break / her ankle

   _____

**C** **Match the questions with the answers.**

_e_ 1. What happened to Jeff?        a. No, he didn't.

___ 2. What was he doing?            b. They had an accident.

___ 3. Did he hurt anything else?    c. Yes, they did.

___ 4. What happened to Paul and Ted?  d. He was painting a window.

___ 5. What were they doing?         e. He hurt his back.

___ 6. Did they go to the hospital?  f. They were driving home.

**D** **Complete the questions. Use *have to*.**

1. A: How often _____ _do I have to take the pills_ _____?

   B: You have to take the pills three times a day.

2. A: _____ with meals?

   B: Yes, you do. Take the pills with breakfast, lunch, and dinner.

3. A: How long _____?

   B: You have to take the pills for two weeks.

# 2 Group work

**A** Work with 2–3 classmates. Write a conversation with 6–8 lines between the receptionist and the patient on the phone. Share your conversation with the class.

A: *Good morning. Dr. Sakura's office.*
B: *I need to make an appointment.*
A: *...*

**B** Interview a partner. Write their answers in your notebook.

1. Do you have allergies? What are you allergic to?
2. Did you have the measles when you were a child? How did you feel?
3. When was the last time you had the flu? How did you feel?
4. Do you have a first-aid kit in your home?

**C** Talk about the answers with your class.

## PROBLEM SOLVING

**A** Listen and read about Julio.

Julio Gonzalez works part-time in a supermarket. Last week, he was operating the forklift when he hurt his arm. He didn't fill out an accident report. He doesn't have health insurance. Now it is difficult for him to do his job because he can't operate the forklift. He's worried about his job and his family.

**B** Work with your classmates. Answer the questions.

1. What is Julio's problem?
2. What can he do? Think of 2 or 3 solutions to his problem.

# UNIT 9

# Money Matters

**FOCUS ON**
- banking and ATMs
- budgets
- reasons with *to* and *because*
- refunds and exchanges
- credit cards

## LESSON 1 Vocabulary

## 1 Learn bank vocabulary

**A** Look at the pictures. Name the amounts of money you see.

 **B** Listen and look at the pictures.

 **C** Listen and repeat the words.

1. bank statement      3. current balance      5. cash           7. credit card bill
2. checking account    4. personal check       6. ATM card       8. savings account

**D** Complete the sentences. Read the sentences to a partner.

1. Peter has $21 in _____ cash _____ in his wallet.

2. Peter wrote a _____ to Green's Garden Store for $350.96.

3. The current balance on Peter's _____ is $540.

4. Peter has $1,800 in his _____.

5. Peter's bank statement says the _____ in his checking account is $850.

6. Peter used his _____ to withdraw $40.

## 2 Talk about using an ATM

**A** Work with your classmates. Match the sentences with the pictures.

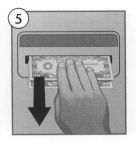  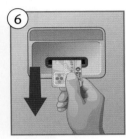

_____ Enter the amount.　　　　　　　__1__ Insert your ATM card for service.

_____ Enter your PIN.　　　　　　　　_____ Remove your card.

_____ Insert the deposit envelope now.　_____ Take your cash.

**B** Listen and check your answers. Then practice the words with a partner.

**C** Mark the sentences T (true) or F (false).

__F__ 1. Peter enters his PIN first and then inserts his ATM card.

_____ 2. Peter deposits $100 in his account.

_____ 3. Peter withdraws $60 from his checking account.

_____ 4. First, Peter takes his cash. Then he removes his ATM card.

**D** Circle the correct words.

1. ( Insert /(Enter)) your PIN.　　　　3. Peter ( deposits / enters ) $100.

2. ( Deposit / Insert ) your card.　　4. He wants to ( withdraw / remove ) $40.

**E** Interview a partner. Ask and answer the questions.

1. Where do you usually see ATMs? Do you use ATMs?
2. Which do people use most—cash, ATM cards, credit cards, or personal checks?

---

**TEST YOURSELF** ✔

Close your book. Write 6 banking words and 4 ATM instructions.
Check your spelling in a dictionary.

# 1 Read about home improvement

**A** Look at the pictures. Tam wants to fix up his kitchen. What do you think he does first? Number the items *1, 2,* or *3.*

_____ compare prices     _____ go shopping     _____ make a list

Ladder—$44.99
**Paint 20% off.**

Deluxe plastic covers
12' x 15'—$14.50
*Buy one get one free!*

Paintbrushes—2 for $15
Paint—$20 a gallon

**Special offer!**
Ladders—$49.99

**B** Listen and read the story.

### Fixing up the Kitchen

Tam wants to fix up his kitchen, but he doesn't have a lot of money. First, he makes a list of everything he'll need. He'll need paint, paintbrushes, a ladder, and some plastic covers. Next, he decides how much he can spend on each item. His total budget is $160. He checks the newspaper for paint sales because he wants to save money. He calls different stores to compare the prices. Finally, he goes to a nearby home improvement store and asks the sales clerk about special offers. The paint is really a bargain there! And the ladder is very cheap, so he decides to buy a new microwave, too!

**C** Check your understanding. Mark the sentences T (true) or F (false).

__F__ 1. Tam can spend $50 on his kitchen.

_____ 2. Tam looks for different ways to save money.

_____ 3. Tam buys an expensive ladder.

_____ 4. Tam buys a microwave.

☑ Evaluate personal budgets; identify ways to save money

## 2 Write about home improvement

**A** Think about your home improvement plans. Complete the paragraph.

I want to _____ my _____.
I will need _____, _____,
and _____. My total budget is $_____.
To save money, I will _____ and _____.
Then I'll go to the _____. Finally,
I'll _____.

**Need help?**

I want to...
paint ___.
buy furniture for ___.
fix up ___.
repair ___.

**B** Read your paragraph to a partner.

## 3 Make a budget

**A** Tam wants to fix up his living room. Listen and complete the budget.
How much money can he spend on the armchair?

| Total budget | $ _____ |
|---|---|
| paint | $30 |
| table lamp | $ |
| area rug | $ |
| armchair (?) | $ |

**B** Listen. Then practice the conversation with a partner.
Use your own ideas.

A: I want to fix up my kitchen.

B: What do you need?

A: I need some paint and a new sink.

B: There are some great bargains out there. Let's go look.

**Need help?**

I need...
furniture.
a new stove.
an area rug.
a lamp.

**TEST YOURSELF** ✔

Close your book. Make a budget for the home improvement plan in 3B.
Write how much you can spend on each item. Tell your partner.

## 1 Learn to give reasons with *to* and *because*

**A** Listen and read. Why does Tam want to return the microwave?

Tam: I'm going to the home improvement store.

Lim: Why are you going there?

Tam: To return the microwave.

Lim: Why are you returning it?

Tam: Because it's too small.

**B** Study the charts. Complete the sentences below.

REASONS WITH *TO* + VERB AND *BECAUSE*

| Reasons with *to* + verb | | |
|---|---|---|
| Tam went to the store | to return | the microwave. the brushes. |

1. Tam went to the store _____ return the microwave.

| Reasons with *because* | | | |
|---|---|---|---|
| He returned | the microwave | because | it was too small. |
| | the brushes | | they were too small. |

2. He returned the microwave _____ it was too small.

3. He returned the brushes because _____ were too small.

**C** Complete the sentences. Use *to* or *because*.

1. Tam went to the store _____ buy some paint.

2. He bought a microwave _____ it was on sale.

3. He went back to the store _____ return the microwave.

4. He wanted a bigger microwave _____ he has a large family.

**D** Complete the sentences. Use *it* or *they*.

1. I wanted to return these paintbrushes because _____ are too small.

2. She didn't like the ladder because _____ is too heavy.

3. He bought two plastic covers because _____ were on sale.

4. They didn't like the paint because _____ was too dark.

☑ Use *because* and infinitives of purpose to give reasons for purchases

## 2 Ask and answer questions with *to* + verb and *because*

**A** Answer the questions. Use *to* + verb and the words in parentheses.

1. **A:** Why did Elsa go to the bank? (withdraw some money)
   **B:** <u>She went to the bank to withdraw some money.</u>

2. **A:** Why did Gina go to the pharmacy? (buy a pain reliever)
   **B:** _____

3. **A:** Why did Mariko go to the home improvement store? (buy a new sink)
   **B:** _____

4. **A:** Why did Jeff need a PIN? (use his ATM card)
   **B:** _____

**B** Answer the questions. Use *because* and the words in parentheses.

1. **A:** Why did Elsa withdraw money? (needs to buy some books)
   **B:** <u>She withdrew money because she needs to buy some books.</u>

2. **A:** Why did Gina buy the pain reliever? (had a headache)
   **B:** _____

3. **A:** Why did Mariko buy a new sink? (wants to fix up her bathroom)
   **B:** _____

4. **A:** Why did Jeff use his ATM card? (wanted to make a deposit)
   **B:** _____

## 3 Practice giving reasons

**A** Think about something you bought. Answer the questions.

1. What did you buy?
2. Why did you buy it/them?

**B** Interview 2 classmates. Ask and answer the questions in 3A.

**A:** *What did you buy?*
**B:** *I bought (a/an/some)...*

**C** Talk about the answers with your class.

### TEST YOURSELF ✔

Write 4 sentences about your classmates' information in 3B. Read your sentences to a partner.

# 1 Learn how to return items to a store

**A** Look at the pictures. Read Lisa's sales receipt. Then circle *a* or *b*.

1. *Get a refund* means _____.
   a. get your money back
   b. choose another item

2. *Exchange* means _____.
   a. get your money back
   b. choose another item

3. Lisa can get a refund _____.
   a. on 10/20
   b. on 11/20

refund

exchange

**Clothing Superstore**

Date 10/15

Coat . . . . . $124.99
Tax . . . . . . . . $8.74
Total . . . . . $133.73

Credit card no.
578XXXXXXXXXXXX

Signature: *Lisa Carter*

Remember! Keep your receipt. You can get a refund or exchange any purchase within 14 days from the original date of purchase.

**B** Listen and read.

| | |
|---|---|
| **Customer:** | Excuse me. I'd like to return this coat. |
| **Clerk:** | Why are you returning it? |
| **Customer:** | Because it doesn't fit. |
| **Clerk:** | OK. Do you have your receipt? |
| **Customer:** | Yes, here it is. |
| **Clerk:** | And would you like a refund, or do you want to exchange it? |
| **Customer:** | I'd like a refund, please. |

**Grammar note**

**Polite expressions with *would like***

**Would like = want**
*Would like* is more polite.
  A: Would you like a refund?
  B: Yes, I would. *or* No, I wouldn't.

**I would like = I'd like**
  I'd like a refund, please.

**C** Listen again and repeat.

**D** Work with a partner. Practice the conversation. Use your own ideas.

**E** Listen to the 3 conversations. Complete the return forms.

①  **Clothing Superstore**
☐ Refund
☐ Exchange
Reason for return:
_____
_____
_____

②  **Clothing Superstore**
☐ Refund
☐ Exchange
Reason for return:
_____
_____
_____

③  **Clothing Superstore**
☐ Refund
☐ Exchange
Reason for return:
_____
_____
_____

## 2 Practice your pronunciation

  **A** **Listen to the sentences. Listen to the pronunciation of *I like* and *I'd like*.**

1. a. I like the blue socks.    2. a. I like new books.
   b. I'd like the blue socks.     b. I'd like new books.

**B** **Listen again and repeat.**

**C** **Listen. Circle *a* or *b*.**

1. a. I like   b. I'd like    3. a. I like   b. I'd like    5. a. I like   b. I'd like
2. a. I like   b. I'd like    4. a. I like   b. I'd like    6. a. I like   b. I'd like

**D** **Write 4 sentences with *I like* or *I'd like*. Read your sentences to a partner. Your partner will say, "You said *I like*" or "You said *I'd like*." Then change roles.**

A: *I'd like a sandwich.*
B: *You said, "I'd like."*

## 3 Real-life math

**A** **Read the receipts. Write the *Amount due* and the *Refund*.**

①
**Clothing Superstore**

Jeans
　　　Return...$24.99

Shoes
　　New item...$34.99

Amount due _____

Jun's receipt

②
**Clothing Superstore**

Sweater
　　　Return...$32.50

T-shirt
　　New item...$15.50

Refund _____

Katura's receipt

**B** **Complete the sentences.**

1. _____ has to pay the store $_____.
2. _____ gets $_____ back from the store.

**TEST YOURSELF** ✔
Role-play a conversation in a store. Partner A: You are a customer with a clothing return. Partner B: You are a store clerk. Use the information from the receipts in 3A.

## 1 Get ready to read

**A** **Read the definitions.**

carry: take or have with you
lend: give to someone for a short period of time
(they will return it later)
lose: be unable to find
protect: make safe

**B** **Work with a partner. Ask and answer the questions.**

1. Are credit cards necessary?
2. What problems do people have with credit cards?

## 2 Read about protecting your credit card

**A** **Read the article.**

# Protecting Your Credit Card

Credit cards are fast and convenient, but no one wants to lose a credit card. That can be a serious problem. Here are some ways to protect your credit card.

- Make a list of your credit card numbers and the expiration dates. Put them in a safe place (not in your wallet).

- When you travel, don't leave your cards in your hotel room or in your car. Don't carry too many cards. Take only the ones you need.

- Some credit cards have PINs. Don't put your PIN in your wallet. Don't write it on the back of your card. Don't use your date of birth for your PIN.

- Don't lend your credit cards to anyone or tell anyone your PINs.

- Don't throw away[1] your receipts. Compare them with your monthly credit card bill. Call the credit card company to report any mistakes immediately.

- When you get a new credit card or close your account, cut your old card into little pieces. That way no one can read the account number.

[1] throw away: put in the trash or garbage

STUDENT
AUDIO

**B** **Listen and read the article again.**

**C** **Find these sentences in the article. What do the underlined words mean? Circle *a* or *b*.**

1. Put <u>them</u> in a safe place.
   a. credit cards
   b. card numbers and expiration dates

2. Take only the <u>ones</u> you need.
   a. credit cards
   b. credit card numbers

3. Don't write <u>it</u> on the back of your card.
   a. your credit card
   b. your PIN

4. Compare <u>them</u> with your credit card bill.
   a. your credit cards
   b. your receipts

**D** **Are these good ideas or bad ideas? Check (✔) the correct boxes.**

|  | Good idea | Bad idea |
|---|---|---|
| 1. Peter uses his date of birth for his PIN because it is easy to remember. |  | ✔ |
| 2. Mary never carries more than one card. She leaves the others at home in a safe place. |  |  |
| 3. Julio uses a credit card, but he never keeps his receipts. |  |  |
| 4. Fatima cuts up her old cards into very small pieces. |  |  |

## 3 Read a bank statement

**A** **Look at the bank statement. Answer the questions.**

1. How much does Peter have in his account now? _____

2. How much did Peter spend in cash and checks this month? _____

3. How much did Peter deposit this month? _____

**STATE BANK**
Page 1 of 3
Account Number: 12345678

PETER CHEN
1343 ELM DR.
GREENBERG, OH 43032

**Account type:** Checking Account

| PREVIOUS BALANCE | CURRENT BALANCE |
|---|---|
| $850.00 | $715.00 |

| CASH WITHDRAWALS | CHECKS | DEPOSITS |
|---|---|---|
| $360.00 | $200.00 | $425.00 |

| DATE | WITHDRAWALS | DEPOSITS | TRANSACTIONS |
|---|---|---|---|
| 11/04 | 47.29 |  | ATM 0755011231001 |
| 11/06 |  | 100.00 | CUSTOMER DEPOSIT |
| 11/07 |  | 100.00 | ONLINE TRANSFER |
| 11/09 | 6.05 |  | ATM 0755011231001 |
| 11/12 | 12.54 |  | ATM 0755011231001 |

**B** **Think about the questions. Talk about the answers with your class.**

1. Is it difficult to save money? Why or why not?
2. Where are some good places to put bank statements and credit card bills?

**BRING IT TO LIFE**

Find an application for a credit card or a bank account and bring it to class. Talk about it with your classmates. What information do you need to complete the application?

## 1 Grammar

**A** Circle the correct words.

1. Maya went to the bank ( because / (to) ) deposit some money.
2. Sheena went to the pharmacy ( because / to ) she needed some pills.
3. Ahmed went to the supermarket ( because / to ) buy some bread.
4. Nesli went to the library ( because / to ) borrow a book.
5. Janet went to the home improvement store ( because / to ) she needed some paint.
6. Nadia went to the train station ( because / to ) she had to buy a train pass.

**B** Unscramble the sentences. Write the conversation.

A: would / like / to return / I / this sweater / Excuse me.
B: is / problem / What / the
A: don't / color / I / like / the
B: a refund / Would / like / or an exchange / you
A: I'd / please / a refund / like

A: _Excuse me. I would like_____.
B: _____?
A: _____.
B: _____?
A: _____.

**C** Complete the sentences and questions. Use the words in parentheses.

1. This microwave is ____too big____. Do you have __a smaller one__? (big, small)
2. This area rug is _____. Do you have _____? (expensive, cheap)
3. This ladder is _____. Do you have _____? (heavy, light)
4. This sofa is _____. Do you have _____? (hard, soft)
5. This lamp is _____. Do you have _____? (tall, short)

**D** Complete the sentences. Use *it* or *them*.

1. I just got a new credit card. Now where did I put _____?
2. Peter got three checks last month. He deposited _____ in the bank.
3. I should put my bills in a safe place. I'll put _____ in the filing cabinet.
4. Oh, no! Where's my receipt? I can't find _____.

## 2 Group work

**A** Work with 2–3 classmates. Write a conversation with 6–8 lines between the people in the picture. Share your conversation with the class.

A: *Excuse me. I'd like to return this radio, please.*
B: *Why are you returning it?*
A: *…*

CUSTOMER SERVICE

**B** Interview 3 classmates. Write their answers in your notebook.

1. When did you return something to a store?
2. What was it?
3. What was wrong with it?
4. Did you get a refund or an exchange?

**C** Talk about the answers with your class.

## PROBLEM SOLVING

**A** Listen and read about Pavel's problem.

Pavel has five credit cards. He uses his credit cards because he doesn't like to carry cash. But he doesn't keep his receipts, and sometimes he spends too much. Then he gets a big credit card bill at the end of the month.

**B** Work with your classmates. Answer the questions.

1. What is Pavel's problem?
2. What should he do? Think of 2 or 3 solutions to his problem.

# Steps to Citizenship

**FOCUS ON**
- citizenship and government officials
- community participation
- *must* and *must not*
- security requests
- U.S. government

## LESSON 1 Vocabulary

## 1 Learn about citizenship

**A** Look at the pictures. Say the dates.

STUDENT AUDIO **B** Listen and look at the pictures.

1

**To become a citizen, you must:**
- ☐ be 18 years old.
- ☐ live in the U.S. for 5 years.
- ☐ take a citizenship test.
- ☐ take an oath of allegiance.

2

PERMANENT RESIDENT CARD
Name **Gomez, Emilia**
A# 000-000-022
Country of Birth
**Mexico**
C1USA0000000000000000022SRC00022
>>>>>>>>>>EMILIAGOMEZ<
5/30/01

3

Application for Naturalization
Name _Emilia Gomez_
Address _____
Date of birth _____
6/23/06

4

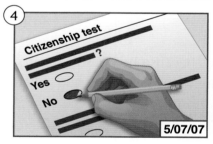
Citizenship test
_____?
Yes ⬭
No ⬭
5/07/07

5

7/18/07

6

PASSPORT
UNITED STATES OF AMERICA
Passport
USA
Gomez, Emilia
Name
20 Oct. 2007
Date of issue
20 Oct. 2017
Date of expiration
10/25/07

STUDENT AUDIO **C** Listen and repeat the words.

1. citizenship requirements
2. resident card
3. application for naturalization
4. citizenship test
5. oath of allegiance
6. passport

**D** Complete the sentences. Read the sentences to a partner.

1. Emilia met all the _____citizenship requirements_____.
2. Emilia got her _____ in May 2001.
3. She filled out the _____ in June 2006.
4. She took a _____ on May 7, 2007.
5. She took the _____ on July 18, 2007.
6. She got her U.S. _____ in October 2007.

## 2 Talk about government officials

**A** **Work with your classmates. Match the words with the pictures.**

Federal Government

State Government

Local Government

| _____ city council | _____ lieutenant governor | _____ U.S. representative |
|---|---|---|
| _____ Congress | _____ mayor | _____ U.S. senator |
| _____ governor | _1_ president | _____ vice president |

**B** **Listen and check your answers. Then practice the words with a partner.**

**C** **Answer the questions about your government officials.**

1. Who is the president of the United States? _____
2. Who is the vice president of the United States? _____
3. Who are the two U.S. senators for your state? _____
4. Who is the U.S. representative for your area? _____
5. Who is the governor of your state? _____
6. Who is the mayor of your city? _____

**D** **Talk about the questions with your classmates.**

1. How can you talk to your state government officials?
2. What problems can you talk to them about?

---

**TEST YOURSELF** ✓

Close your book. Write 4 words or phrases about citizenship and 5 words
for government officials. Check your spelling in a dictionary.

# 1 Read about participating in the community

**A** Look at the pictures. Find these people in the pictures.

> volunteers    city council members    mayor

**B** Listen and read the story.

### Helping the Community

Sharma's children go to Riverdale High School. The school has a problem. The city is cutting the budget, and now there isn't enough money for books. Sharma went to a meeting of the Parent-Teacher Association (PTA). The parents and teachers decided to do two things:

- Have a bake sale to raise money.
- Go to the next city council meeting.

Volunteers made cookies and sold them at the bake sale. They raised over $500. Then Sharma and some PTA members went to the city council meeting. They told the council members, "We need books for our school." Finally, Sharma wrote a letter to the mayor. She wrote, "Our schools need more money for books." The mayor and council members promised to think about the problem.

**C** Check your understanding. Mark the sentences T (true) or F (false).

___T___ 1. Sharma is a parent.

_____ 2. At the city council meeting, the PTA sold cookies.

_____ 3. At the bake sale, the volunteers raised under $500.

_____ 4. Sharma wrote a letter to the mayor.

## 2 Write about a community problem

**A** Think about a problem in your community. Answer the questions.
Write your answers in a paragraph.

¹ What is the problem? ² Who can you talk to about the problem? ³ What can you do about the problem? (Give two ideas.) ⁴ Who can you call or write to?

_____

_Our community has a problem._____

_____

_____

_____

_____

> **Need help?**
>
> **Problems**
> Our community needs...
>   a stop sign.
>   a street light.
>   a clean park.

**B** Read your paragraph to a partner. Think of some other solutions to the problem.

## 3 Understand a flyer

**A** Look at the PTA News flyer. Listen and write the missing information.

**B** Listen. Then practice the conversation with a partner. Use the information from the PTA News.

A: What's happening on October 10th?
B: There's an Open House.
A: Oh, yes. That's right. Are you going to go?
B: Yes, I want to meet the teachers.

**Hillside High School**
**PTA NEWS**

**Meet the teachers!**
**Open House**
Date: October 10th    Time: _7 p.m.–9 p.m._
Call Mr. Wu at _____.

**Help clean up our school!**
**Parent-Student Action Meeting**
Date: _____ Time: 8 a.m.–2 p.m.
Call Mr. Perez at _____.

**Raise money for books!**
**Student Art Show**
Date: _____ Time: _____
Call Mrs. Mason at 555-3989.

> **TEST YOURSELF** ✔
>
> Close your book. Write about 3 ways to participate in your community. Tell a partner.

## 1 Learn *must* and *must not*

**A** Listen and look at the pictures. Do you always follow these rules?

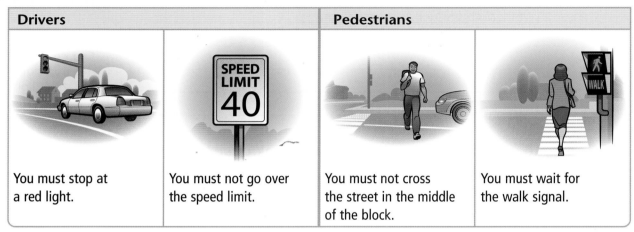

| Drivers | | Pedestrians | |
|---|---|---|---|
| You must stop at a red light. | You must not go over the speed limit. | You must not cross the street in the middle of the block. | You must wait for the walk signal. |

**B** Study the grammar charts. Complete the sentences below.

*MUST AND MUST NOT*

**Affirmative statements**

| I | | | We | | |
|---|---|---|---|---|---|
| You | must | stop. | You | must | stop. |
| He She | | | They | | |

1. He _____ stop.     2. You must _____.

**Negative statements**

| I | | | We | | |
|---|---|---|---|---|---|
| You | must not | cross here. | You | must not | cross here. |
| He She | | | They | | |

3. She must _____ cross here.     4. We _____ not _____ here.

**C** Complete the sentences. Use *must (not)* and the verbs in parentheses.

1. Drivers _____*must stop*_____ at a red light. (stop)

2. Drivers _____ on the sidewalk. (drive)

3. Pedestrians _____ for the walk signal. (wait)

4. Pedestrians _____ in the street. (walk)

☑ Use *must* for obligation to describe community and transportation rules

## 2 Statements with *must* and *must not*

**A** Read the rules. Mark the sentences T (true) or F (false). Change the false sentences. Make them true.

**Rules on the bus:**

Don't talk to the bus driver.
Stand behind the yellow line.
No food or drink.
No radios.
Exact change only.

_F_ 1. Passengers must ^not talk to the driver.

____ 2. Passengers must stand behind the yellow line.

____ 3. Passengers must eat and drink on the bus.

____ 4. Passengers must listen to radios.

____ 5. Passengers must give the driver exact change.

**B** Look at the signs. Write sentences with *must* or *must not*.

| CROSS AT CORNER ONLY | NO PARKING HERE | ENTER HERE | NO RIGHT TURN |

1. _You must cross at the corner._

2. _____

3. _____

4. _____

## 3 Practice using *must* and *must not*

**A** Think of one new rule for your community. Write it in the chart.

| | New rules for our community |
|---|---|
| My idea | |
| Classmate 1 | |
| Classmate 2 | |

**B** Ask 2 classmates about their rules. Write them in the chart.

A: *What is your new rule for our community?*
B: *My new rule is…*

**C** Talk about the rules with your class.

**TEST YOURSELF** ✓

Write 3 new rules for your community or classroom. Read your rules to a partner.
*You must not be late for class.*

## 1 Learn how to respond to police and security officers

**A** Look at the pictures. Which kinds of identification do you have?

driver's license and registration     passport     photo ID     train pass

**B** Listen and read.

**Officer:** Good afternoon. May I see your license and registration, please?
**Driver:** Of course. Here they are.
**Officer:** Did you know that your left taillight is broken?
**Driver:** No, I didn't. I'll take care of it right away.
**Officer:** OK. Have a good day.

**C** Listen again and repeat.

**D** Work with a partner. Practice the conversation. Use the situations in the chart below.

A: *Good afternoon. May I see your passport, please?*
B: *Of course…*

| Official | May I see your...? | Problem |
|---|---|---|
| immigration officer | passport | There is no signature. |
| security guard | photo ID | The photo is too old. |
| train conductor | train pass | Your pass expired last week. |

**E** Listen to the 3 conversations. Check (✔) the problem in each conversation.

1. ☐ parking     ☐ speeding     ☐ driving on the sidewalk
2. ☐ no seat belt     ☐ no taillight     ☐ no license
3. ☐ didn't slow down     ☐ didn't turn     ☐ didn't stop

## 2 Practice using *must* and *should*

**A** Read the rules and advice in the chart. Do you use *should* for rules or for advice?

| Rules *(It's the law!)* | Advice *(It's a good idea.)* |
|---|---|
| You must wear a seat belt. | You should check your car engine regularly. |
| You must not drink alcohol and drive. | You should not play loud music in your car. |

**B** Is it the law? Complete the sentences. Use *must (not)* or *should (not)*.

1. You _____should_____ wash your car every month.
2. You _____ have your car registration.
3. You _____ drive on the sidewalk.
4. You _____ eat and drive at the same time.
5. You _____ drive without your license.

**C** Compare your answers with a partner.


## 3 Real-life math

**A** Read about the traffic problems. Complete the sentences. Write numbers for the words in parentheses.

This is a list of traffic violations in one year for one state in the United States. About six million people live in this state.

1. The police gave __139,500__ tickets to people for speeding.
   (one hundred thirty-nine thousand five hundred)

2. They stopped _____ people because they weren't wearing seat belts.
   (sixty-one thousand five hundred thirty-eight)

3. Police gave tickets to _____ people because they didn't stop at
   stop signs. (one thousand seven hundred twenty-five)

4. Police stopped _____ people because they weren't driving on the
   right side of the road. (two thousand one hundred eighty-four)

**B** Read the sentences to a partner.

**TEST YOURSELF** ✔
Role-play a conversation with a security guard or other official. Partner A:
You are the security guard. Partner B: You are talking to the security guard
about a problem with your ID. Then change roles.

## 1 Get ready to read

**A** **Read the definitions.**

**branch:** a part of the government or other organization
**court:** place where a judge works
**judge:** a person who makes decisions about the law

**B** **Write one thing you think the president does. Talk about your ideas with your classmates.**

## 2 Read about the branches of the U.S. government

**A** **Read the article.**

# The Three Branches of Government

There are three branches of the U.S. government: the Executive Branch, the Legislative Branch, and the Judicial Branch.

### The Executive Branch

The president, the vice president, and the Cabinet are in the executive branch. The president is the leader of the country. He signs new laws. The vice president helps the president. If the president dies, the vice president becomes president. The members of the Cabinet are leaders of government departments like the Department of Education. They advise[1] the president.

### The Legislative Branch

Congress is in the legislative branch. Congress has two parts: the Senate and the House of Representatives. Congress makes new laws for the country. There are 100 senators in the Senate and 435 representatives in the House of Representatives.

### The Judicial Branch

The Supreme Court and the federal courts are in the judicial branch. The courts explain the laws. The Supreme Court is the highest court in the United States. There are nine judges on the Supreme Court.

[1]advise: tell someone what they should do; give advice

STUDENT
AUDIO

**B** **Listen and read the article again.**

 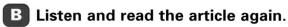

**C** These sentences are false. Make them true.

                  *president*

1. The ~~vice president~~ is the leader of the executive branch of government.

2. The president makes new laws for the country.

3. The Cabinet is part of the judicial branch.

4. There are 100 representatives in the House of Representatives.

5. There are six judges on the Supreme Court.

**D** Complete the sentences. Use the words in the box.

| advise    laws    judges    branches    ~~leader~~ |
| --- |

1. The president is the _____ *leader* _____ of the country.

2. The president signs new _____.

3. The government has three _____.

4. The members of the Cabinet _____ the president.

5. The Supreme Court has nine _____.

# 3 Read about government officials

**A** Read the chart. Circle the correct years in the sentences below.

|  | President | U.S. Senator | U.S. Representative | Supreme Court Judge |
| --- | --- | --- | --- | --- |
| How long is a term? | four years | six years | two years | for life* |
| How many terms can he or she serve? | two terms | no limit | no limit | |

*The president chooses the Supreme Court judges. They are not elected by the people. The judges are on the Supreme Court until they die or decide to retire.

1. Senator Jones was elected in 1998. His term ended in ( 2000 / 2004 ).

2. Representative Smith was elected in 2004. His term ended in ( 2006 / 2010 ).

3. The president was elected in 2002. His term ended in ( 2006 / 2008 ).

**B** Think about the questions. Talk about the answers with your class.

1. Would you like to be a government official? Why or why not?

2. What are three questions you would like to ask the president?

**BRING IT TO LIFE**

Brainstorm a list of questions about the U.S. government with your classmates. Find the answer to one question on the Internet or in the library. Talk about the answers with your class.

## 1 Grammar

**A** Read the signs. Complete the sentences. Use *must (not)*.

| **BUS** No smoking. Stand behind the yellow line. | **Library** Please return books on time. | **MUSEUM** No cameras. | **Bookstore** No food or drink. |

1. You _____ must not _____ smoke on the bus.
2. You _____ stand behind the yellow line on the bus.
3. You _____ return the library books on time.
4. You _____ take cameras into the museum.
5. You _____ eat or drink in the bookstore.

**B** Complete the sentences. Use *must* or *should*.

RULES AND ADVICE FOR DRIVERS:

1. You _____ have a road map in your car.
2. You _____ have taillights on your car.
3. You _____ wash your car often.
4. You _____ have a driver's license.

**C** Write questions for these answers. Use *have to* + verb.

1. **A:** _Do we have to take the citizenship test?_
   **B:** Yes, you must take the citizenship test.
2. **A:** _____
   **B:** Yes, he has to be 18 years old to apply for citizenship.
3. **A:** _____
   **B:** Yes, they must take the oath of allegiance.

> **Grammar note**
>
> **Questions with *have to***
>
> In the U.S., people usually don't ask questions with *must*:
> ~~Must we go now?~~
>
> They use *have to*:
> Do we have to go now?

**D** Unscramble the questions.

1. open / your bag / Could / please / you

   _____

2. please / I / see / passport / your / Can

   _____

3. see / May / photo ID / I / please / your

   _____

> **Need help?**
>
> **Polite requests**
> You can use *may*, *could*, or *can* for polite requests.
>
> *May* and *could* are more formal than *can*.

# 2 Group work

**A** Work with 2–3 classmates. Write a conversation of 6–8 lines between the people in the picture. Share your conversation with the class.

A: *May I see your license and registration, please?*

B: *Of course, Officer…*

**B** Interview 3 classmates about their participation in the community. Check (✔) their answers in the chart.

A: *How do you participate in the community?*

B: *Well, I volunteer at…*

|  | Classmate 1 | Classmate 2 | Classmate 3 |
|---|---|---|---|
| Volunteer |  |  |  |
| Go to city council meetings |  |  |  |
| Go to PTA meetings |  |  |  |
| Read a local newspaper |  |  |  |
| Other: _____ |  |  |  |

**C** Talk about the answers with your class.

*Tam often goes to city council meetings.*

## PROBLEM SOLVING

**A** Listen and read about Kamali's problem.

Kamali was driving past a school last week at 45 miles per hour. The speed limit there is 20 miles per hour. A police officer stopped him and gave him a ticket for speeding. He has to pay $150 for the ticket, but he doesn't have the money right now.

**B** Work with your classmates. Answer the questions.

1. What is Kamali's problem?
2. What can he do? Think of 2 or 3 solutions to his problem.

# Deal with Difficulties

**FOCUS ON**
- emergencies and natural disasters
- emergency situations and services
- the present and past
- 911 calls
- emergency safety procedures

**LESSON 1** Vocabulary

## 1 Learn about crimes and emergencies

**A** Look at the pictures. Name the locations of the crimes and emergencies.

STUDENT
AUDIO **B** Listen and look at the pictures.

STUDENT
AUDIO **C** Listen and repeat the words.

1. robbery    2. accident    3. mugging    4. blackout    5. explosion    6. vandalism

**D** Complete the sentences. Read the sentences to a partner.

1. There was an _____accident_____ on the highway.
2. There was a _____ in the store.
3. There was _____ at the corner of Park Street and 3rd Avenue.
4. There was an _____ at the factory.
5. There was a _____ in front of the bank.
6. There was a _____ in the subway.

## 2 Talk about natural disasters

### A Work with your classmates. Match the words with the pictures.

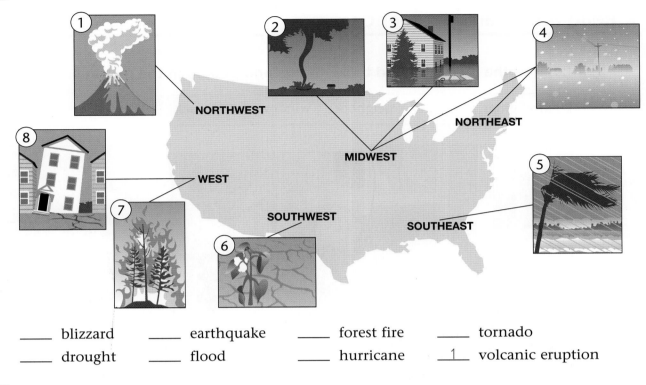

NORTHWEST

NORTHEAST

MIDWEST

WEST

SOUTHWEST

SOUTHEAST

| _____ blizzard | _____ earthquake | _____ forest fire | _____ tornado |
| _____ drought | _____ flood | _____ hurricane | __1__ volcanic eruption |

STUDENT AUDIO

### B Listen and check your answers. Then practice the words with a partner.

### C Complete the sentences.

1. 1974: On April 3rd–4th, there were 148 _____ tornadoes _____ in the Midwest.
2. 1930s: The Midwest had a ten-year _____. There was very little rain.
3. 1980: Fire and smoke came from a _____ at Mount St. Helens.
4. 2005: Water from a _____ covered roads and bridges in New Jersey.
5. 1978: Four feet of snow fell during a _____ in the Northeast.
6. 1992: A _____ in Florida had winds of 145 miles per hour.
7. 1906: Many buildings fell during an _____ in San Francisco.
8. 1956: In California, a _____ burned 40,000 acres of forest.

### D Interview a partner. Ask and answer the questions.

1. What areas of the U.S. do hurricanes, earthquakes, and tornadoes occur in?
2. What emergencies or natural disasters happen in your city or state?

### TEST YOURSELF ✔

Close your book. Write 5 crimes or emergencies and 5 natural disasters.
Check your spelling in a dictionary.

# 1 Read about an emergency

**A**   **Look at the pictures. Find these things and people in the pictures.**

| firefighter    smoke    neighbor    window    fire truck |

**B**   **Listen and read the story.**

### A Helpful Neighbor

My neighbor George likes to do yard work, and he likes to cook. Sometimes he does both at the same time! Last week, he was cooking some sausages. Then he went out to the front yard. I was standing by my window when I saw smoke. It was coming out of George's kitchen window. I immediately called 911. Then I ran to the house and banged on the back door. No answer!

The fire truck arrived five minutes later. George was doing yard work in front of the house. When I went to the front of the house, he was talking to a firefighter. "Where's the fire?" George asked. "In your kitchen!" I said. Luckily, the fire wasn't serious, but the kitchen walls were black from the smoke.

George will never try to cook and do yard work at the same time again.

**C**   **Check your understanding. Number the sentences in the correct order.**

_____ The firefighters came to George's house.

_____ A fire started in George's kitchen.

_____ George went out to the front yard.

_____ George's neighbor called 911.

__1__ George was cooking sausages.

## 2 Write about an emergency

**A** Choose one picture. Imagine you saw this emergency. Think about what happened. Complete the paragraph.

> **Need help?**
>
> I called...
>   an ambulance.
>   911.
>   the fire department.
>   the police.

Last week, I was _____ when I saw _____.

I immediately called _____. Then I _____.

The _____ arrived _____ minutes later.

**B** Read your paragraph to a partner. Who did your partner call?

## 3 Talk about an emergency

**A** Listen. Complete the forms with the emergencies.

**①Emergency Report**
Name: _Al Andrews_
Place: _34th and West St._
Emergency: _____
_____

**②Emergency Report**
Name: _Parvin Mulla_
Place: _Subway Station_
Emergency: _____
_____

**③Emergency Report**
Name: _Ella Chapman_
Place: _238 Westside Ave._
Emergency: _____
_____

**B** Listen. Then practice the conversation with a partner. Use the forms in 3A.

A: Did you hear about George?

B: What happened?

A: He had a fire in his kitchen.

B: Oh, that's terrible. Is he OK?

A: Yes, he's fine.

> **TEST YOURSELF** ✔
> Close your book. Write about 2 emergencies that happened in the news this
> week or last week. Tell a partner.
> *There was a fire on...*

## 1 Review present and past verb forms

**A** **Look at the picture and read Ramiro's story. Then answer the questions.**

1. What was the problem?
2. Did Ramiro go to work?

I usually drive to work. I leave my house at 8 a.m. When I left for work yesterday, it was raining a lot. There was a flood under the bridge on First Avenue. Some police officers were helping drivers to get out of their cars. I decided to go home! I didn't go to work. Floods can be dangerous!

**B** **Study the chart.**

### PRESENT AND PAST VERB FORMS

|  | Affirmative statements | Negative statements |
|---|---|---|
| Simple present | I usually drive to work.<br>He usually drives to work. | I don't drive every day.<br>He doesn't drive every day. |
| Simple past | I drove to work last week.<br>He left at 8 a.m. | I didn't drive to work yesterday.<br>He didn't leave at 7 a.m. |
| Past continuous | It was raining.<br>The officers were helping drivers. | It wasn't snowing.<br>They weren't driving to work. |

**C** **Answer the questions about Ramiro. Use the information in 1A.**

1. How does Ramiro usually get to work?
   _He usually drives to work._

2. What time did he leave for work yesterday?
   _____

3. What was the weather like?
   _____

4. What were the police officers doing?
   _____

5. What did Ramiro do?
   _____

## 2 Review questions and answers in the present and past

### A Study the chart.

| | Information questions | Yes/No questions |
|---|---|---|
| Simple present | **A:** How does he usually go to work? <br> **B:** He usually drives. | **A:** Does he usually drive to work? <br> **B:** Yes, he does. |
| Simple past | **A:** How did she go to work yesterday? <br> **B:** She drove. | **A:** Did she drive to work yesterday? <br> **B:** No, she didn't. |
| Past continuous | **A:** What were the officers doing? <br> **B:** They were helping drivers. | **A:** Was it raining? <br> **B:** Yes, it was. |

### B Complete the conversation. Use present or past forms of the verbs in parentheses.

Reporter: _____Do_____ you usually _____drive_____ to work? (drive)

Moy: No, I don't. I usually _____. (walk)

Reporter: What time _____ you _____ for work yesterday? (leave)

Moy: I _____ at 9:00 in the morning. (leave)

Reporter: What _____ you _____ at Third Street? (see)

Moy: An accident. A police officer _____ to the drivers. (talk)

Reporter: Were the drivers hurt?

Moy: No, they _____. It wasn't a serious accident. (be, not)

## 3 Practice using the present and the past

### A Think of one day of the week. Complete each question with this day. Write answers for each question in your notebook.

1. What do you usually do on _____?

2. What did you do last _____?

3. What were you doing at 3 p.m. last _____?

### B Interview a partner. Ask and answer the questions in 3A.

A: *What do you usually do on Friday?*

B: *I usually go to work. In the evening, I have dinner with a friend.*

### C Talk about the answers with your class.

**TEST YOURSELF** ✔

Write 3 sentences about you and 3 sentences about your partner. Use the information in 3A and 3B.

## 1 Learn how to make a 911 call

  **A** **Which of these things are 911 emergencies? Mark the emergencies _E_. Mark the non-emergencies _NE_. Then listen and check.**

1. Police
   NE  a stolen bicycle
   ____  a robbery

2. Fire
   ____  a fire or smoke
   ____  a cat in a tree

3. Medical
   ____  a small cut or burn
   ____  a broken leg

  **B** **Listen and read.**

| | |
|---|---|
| **Operator:** | 911. What's your emergency? |
| **Man:** | It's a medical emergency. |
| **Operator:** | Where are you? |
| **Man:** | I'm at 23 Oakfield Road at A & B Construction Company. |
| **Operator:** | What happened? |
| **Man:** | My co-worker fell and hurt her leg. |
| **Operator:** | What number are you calling from? |
| **Man:** | (219) 555-1702. |

**C** **Listen again and repeat.**

**D** **Work with a partner. Practice the conversation. Use your own ideas.**

> **Need help?**
>
> **911 emergencies**
> It's a police emergency.
> It's a medical emergency.
> There's a fire.

  **E** **Listen to the 2 conversations. Circle the correct information in the forms.**

① **EMERGENCY**

Type of emergency:
police / medical / fire

Place:
home / work / street

② **EMERGENCY**

Type of emergency:
police / medical / fire

Place:
home / work / street

**F** **Listen again. What are the problems?**

## 2 Practice your pronunciation

**A** Listen and say the words in the chart. Listen for the number of syllables and the stressed syllables.

| Words | Syllables | Stressed syllable |
|---|---|---|
| 1. áccident | 3 | first |
| 2. impórtant | 3 | second |
| 3. informátion | 4 | third |

**B** Listen and say the words. Put a dot (•) over each stressed syllable. Complete the chart.

| Words | Syllables | Stressed syllable |
|---|---|---|
| 1. óperator | 4 | first |
| 2. ambulance | | |
| 3. description | | |
| 4. immediate | | |

**C** Practice saying the words in 2A and 2B with a partner.

## 3 Real-life math

**A** Read the graph. Answer the questions.

1. What is the main cause of accidents in the home?
2. How many people had accidents in each situation?
3. Which caused more accidents, knives or scissors?

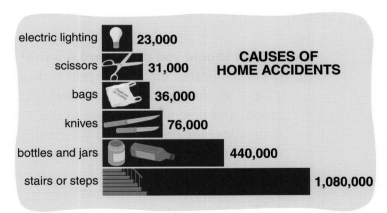

CAUSES OF HOME ACCIDENTS

electric lighting 23,000
scissors 31,000
bags 36,000
knives 76,000
bottles and jars 440,000
stairs or steps 1,080,000

Source: Injury Facts® 2004 Edition *published by National Safety Council®*

**B** How did you find the answers? Tell a partner.

**TEST YOURSELF** ✓

Role-play a 911 call. Partner A: You see an emergency. Call 911. Partner B: Answer your partner's call. Ask questions about the emergency. Then change roles.

## 1 Get ready to read

**A** Read the definitions.

evacuate: leave a place because it is dangerous
prepare: get ready for something
rescue: save someone from a dangerous situation

**B** Work with a partner. Check (✔) the things you do to prepare for an emergency.

☐ Find the emergency exit.   ☐ Turn off the electricity.
☐ Listen to the news.   ☐ Prepare an emergency kit.
☐ Talk to your family.   ☐ Read safety information.

## 2 Read about emergency safety procedures

**A** Read the article.

### BE READY FOR AN EMERGENCY

An emergency can happen at any time. It is a good idea to prepare for an emergency before it happens. For example, prepare an emergency kit. Learn the location of emergency exits at work and at school. Talk with your family about what to do in an emergency.

| **What should you do if there is a fire?** | **What should you do if there is a flood?** |
| --- | --- |
| Go to the nearest emergency exit. Is there a lot of smoke? Put a wet towel over your mouth and nose and stay close to the floor. Close the doors behind you to stop the fire. Put wet towels at the bottom of doors to stop the smoke. Before you open a door, touch it. Is it hot? Don't open it. Find another exit or wait for emergency services to rescue you. | Listen to the news for flood warnings. Turn off the electricity and the gas. Close all the windows. Move your valuables[1] off the floor or to the second floor of your home. Fill bathtubs and sinks with clean water for drinking. Be ready to evacuate your home. |

[1]valuables: expensive or important things

STUDENT
AUDIO

**B** Listen and read the article again.

**C** Choose the correct words. Circle *a* or *b*.

1. In a fire, you should _____.
   a. turn off the electricity
   b. go to an emergency exit

2. In a fire, you should _____.
   a. close doors
   b. fill sinks with clean water

3. In a flood, you should _____.
   a. turn on the electricity
   b. turn off the gas

4. In a flood, you should _____.
   a. be ready to evacuate
   b. stay in your kitchen

**D** Complete the sentences. Use the words in the box.

| evacuate | valuables | prepare | rescue |
|---|---|---|---|

1. To be ready for an emergency, you should _____ an emergency kit.
2. In a serious flood, you should move your _____ off the floor.
3. In an emergency, you may have to _____ your home.
4. In a fire, you might have to wait for emergency services to _____ you.

# 3 Read an emergency kit checklist

**A** Read the emergency kit checklist. Check (✔) the items you have at home.

### Emergency Kit Checklist

☐ food      ☐ water      ☐ blanket
☐ first-aid kit ☐ radio    ☐ flashlight
☐ knife     ☐ batteries   ☐ can opener

**B** Think about the questions. Talk about the answers with your class.

1. Why do you need the items in the checklist? What is each item for?
2. Add two of the items below to your emergency kit. Tell your partner why they are important.

| newspaper | medicine | candy | hot water bottle | extra clothes |
|---|---|---|---|---|

**BRING IT TO LIFE**

Choose an emergency that happens in your state: for example, a hurricane. Find information on the Internet or in the library about the safety procedures for this emergency. Talk about the information with your class.

## 1 Grammar

**A** Circle the correct words.

1. It didn't ( **rain** / rained ) last week.
2. We ( stand / were standing ) in the park when we saw the lightning.
3. I always ( was driving / drive ) carefully on icy roads.
4. It was too foggy. He ( didn't see / doesn't see ) the other car.
5. Every year forest fires ( burn / were burning ) thousands of trees.
6. It ( snowed / was snowing ) when I looked out the window.

**B** Unscramble the questions.

1. did / go / to / How / you / yesterday / work
   _How did you go to work yesterday?_

2. drive / she / every day / Does / to school
   _____

3. they / Where / were / this morning / going
   _____

4. they / to the station / Do / go / every morning
   _____

5. see / you / the accident / Did / yesterday
   _____

6. prepare / for a flood / do / How / you
   _____

**C** Complete the questions for each answer.

1. A: What _____ _were you waiting for_ _____?
   B: I was waiting for <u>my bus</u>.

2. A: What time _____?
   B: I usually start work <u>at 8 a.m.</u>

3. A: When _____?
   B: I saw the tornado <u>at 7:30 a.m.</u>

4. A: Where _____?
   B: I went <u>into the basement</u>.

5. A: When _____?
   B: He usually goes to the movies <u>on Saturday</u>.

# 2 Group work

**A** Work with 2–3 classmates. Write 6–8 sentences about the picture. Talk about your sentences with the class.

*It is very cold. The people…*

**B** What should you do in an emergency? Choose an emergency below. Interview 3 classmates. Write their ideas in the chart.

| an earthquake     a fire     a flood     a tornado     a hurricane |
| --- |

A: *What should we do in a hurricane?*
B: *I think we should stay in the building.*

| What should we do in _____? | |
| --- | --- |
| **Classmates' names** | **Ideas** |
| 1. | |
| 2. | |
| 3. | |

**C** Talk about your ideas with the class.

## PROBLEM SOLVING

**A** Listen and read about Min's problem.

It's a clear, sunny day, but Min heard a hurricane warning for her area on the news. Her husband is in Mexico for business, her kids are at school, and she doesn't have a car. Min's at home alone, and she's worried about her house.

**B** Work with your classmates. Answer the questions.

1. What is Min's problem?
2. What should she do? Think of 2 or 3 solutions to her problem.

# Take the Day Off

**FOCUS ON**
- recreation and entertainment
- automated phone menus
- the superlative
- giving opinions
- travel in the U.S.

## LESSON **1**   Vocabulary

### **1** Learn about recreational activities

**A**  **Look at the pictures. Name the months of the year.**

**B**  **Listen and look at the pictures**.

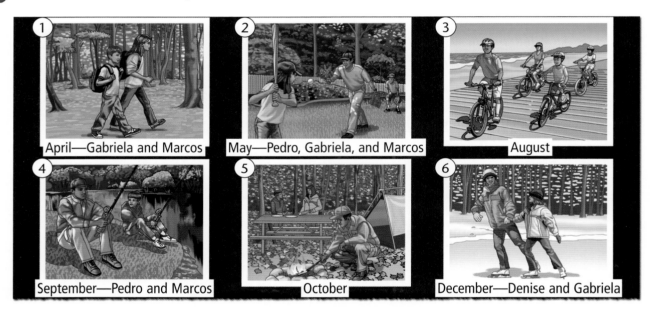

| 1 April—Gabriela and Marcos | 2 May—Pedro, Gabriela, and Marcos | 3 August |
| 4 September—Pedro and Marcos | 5 October | 6 December—Denise and Gabriela |

**C**  **Listen and repeat the words.**

1. go hiking       3. go biking       5. go camping
2. play softball   4. go fishing      6. go skating

**D**  **Complete the sentences. Read the sentences to a partner.**

1. The family likes to _____go camping_____ in October.
2. They sometimes _____ in August.
3. Gabriela and Marcos like to _____ in April.
4. Denise and Gabriela always _____ in December.
5. Pedro and Marcos usually _____ in September.
6. Pedro and the children always _____ in May.

☑ **Identify recreational activities and entertainment genres**

## **2** Talk about entertainment

**A** Work with your classmates. Match the words with the picture.

| | | |
|---|---|---|
| ____ action | ____ educational | ____ romantic |
| __1__ computer game | ____ horror | ____ science fiction |
| ____ DVD | ____ mystery | ____ video cassette |

**B** Listen and check your answers. Then practice the words with a partner.

**C** Work with a partner. Answer questions about the picture.

1. What kind of movie is *Lost in Paris?* _____ romantic _____
2. What is the title of the horror movie? _____
3. What is the title of the action game? _____
4. What kind of book is *The Stolen Diamond?* _____
5. What is the title of the educational program? _____

**D** Work with a partner. Practice the conversation. Use your own ideas.

**A:** What do you do to relax?

**B:** I like to go biking. How about you?

**A:** I like to watch action movies.

**TEST YOURSELF** ✔

Close your book. Write 8 words for recreation and entertainment. Check your spelling in a dictionary.

# 1 Read about weekend activities

**A** Look at the pictures. What do you think Denise and her family will do this weekend? Check (✔) your ideas.

- ☐ go to a movie
- ☐ go shopping
- ☐ watch sports
- ☐ go to the zoo
- ☐ listen to music
- ☐ go to a museum

**B** Listen and read the story.

### Denise's Weekend

This weekend is a three-day weekend. It's going to be fun to spend time with my family. On Saturday, my daughter Gabriela has a soccer game with her school team, and we are all going to watch. Pedro and I like to talk with the other parents. Sometimes we talk too much and forget to watch the game. Gabriela gets really upset when we do that.

On Sunday, we're planning to visit the Science Museum. There is a new show about dinosaurs. Our son, Marcos, loves dinosaurs. Sunday is the cheapest day to go to the museum because it's Family Day. We can buy one special ticket for the whole family for just $22.

On Monday, we're going to go to the movies. Pedro and the children want to see the new horror movie. I don't like horror movies, but I guess they're better than action movies. Next week I get to choose the movie!

**C** Check your understanding. Mark the sentences T (true) or F (false).

___F___ 1. Denise is going to stay home this weekend.

_____ 2. Gabriela is going to play soccer.

_____ 3. Denise and her family can visit the museum on Sunday for free.

_____ 4. They're going to a movie about dinosaurs.

## 2 Write about weekend plans

**A** Think about your weekend plans with your family or friends. Answer the questions. Write your answers in a paragraph.

¹ Where are you going to go on Saturday? ² Who are you going to go with? ³ What are you going to do? ⁴ Where are you going to go on Sunday? ⁵ What are you going to do?

_On Saturday, I am going to go_ _____

_____

_____

_____

**B** Read your paragraph to a partner. Ask for more information about your partner's plans.

## 3 Listen and respond to a recorded phone message

**A** Listen to the recorded message. Answer the questions. Write the numbers.

1. Which number tells you about ticket prices? ____
2. Which number gives you the operator? ____
3. Which number gives you movie times? ____
4. You want to listen to the message again. Which number do you press? ____
5. Which number tells you the theater locations? ____

star key

pound key

**B** Listen. Then practice the conversation with a partner. Use your own ideas.

A: Did you find out what's playing at the movies?

B: Yes, they're showing *Endless Winter* and *Dangerous Drivers*.

A: Let's go to see *Dangerous Drivers*! When does it start?

B: The first show is at 6:00. Then it's showing again at 8:30.

A: Let's go to the show at 6:00.

---

**TEST YOURSELF** ✔

Close your book. Write 3 things you plan to do this weekend. Tell a partner about them.

## 1 Learn the superlative

**A** Look at the movies of the year. Which movies would you like to see?

**B** Study the chart.

### THE SUPERLATIVE

| | Adjective | Superlative | Notes |
|---|---|---|---|
| One syllable | long<br>large<br>sad | the longest<br>the largest<br>the saddest | Add -est or -st. For words like sad, double the final consonant. |
| Ending in -y | funny<br>scary | the funniest<br>the scariest | Change y to i and add -est. |
| Two or more syllables | exciting<br>famous | the most exciting<br>the most famous | Put the most in front of the adjective. |
| Irregular forms | good<br>bad | the best<br>the worst | |

**C** Complete the sentences. Use the superlative of the adjectives in parentheses.

1. *Goodbye for Now* was _____the saddest_____ movie this year. (sad)

2. *Nightmare City* was _____ movie this year. (scary)

3. Paul Knight was _____ actor in *Endless Winter*. (famous)

4. What was _____ movie this year? (good)

5. *Monsters 2* was definitely _____ movie this year. (bad)

## 2 Ask and answer questions with the superlative

**A** Complete the questions about Ben's list. Use the superlative of the adjectives in the advertisment.

1. What is _____the most popular_____ sport according to Ben's List?
2. Where is _____ hotel in the U.S.?
3. What is _____ sport in the U.S.?
4. What is _____ type of vacation in the U.S.?

> ### BEN'S LIST OF "THE MOST" AND "THE BEST" IN THE U.S.
>
> ✔ **POPULAR SPORT**
> *Football, of course!*
>
> ✔ **EXPENSIVE HOTEL**
> *In Las Vegas!*
>
> ✔ **SCARY SPORT**
> *Bungee-jumping!*
> *Try it!*
>
> ✔ **CHEAP VACATION**
> *Camping!*

**B** Answer the questions. Use the opinions in Ben's List.

1. _According to Ben, the most popular sport in the U.S. is football._
2. _____
3. _____
4. _____

## 3 Practice using the superlative

**A** Complete the questions. Write your answers in your notebook.

1. Who is _____the most famous movie star_____? (famous movie star)
2. Who is _____? (famous football player)
3. What is _____? (funny TV show)
4. What is _____? (popular sport)
5. What is _____? (good music)

**B** Interview a partner. Ask and answer the questions in 3A.

A: *Who is the most famous movie star?*
B: *I think the most famous movie star is…*

**C** Talk about the answers with your class.

**TEST YOURSELF** ✔

Write 6 sentences about your opinions and your partner's opinions of popular entertainment. Use the information in 3A and 3B.

## 1 Learn how to ask for and give opinions

**A** Look at the pictures. Which things do you do most often? Number them from 1 (often) to 4 (not very often).

_____ watch sports    _____ watch TV shows    _____ go to concerts    _____ eat out

**B** Listen and read.

**Sheryl:** How was the baseball game last night?

**Brian:** It was great! Pete Ramirez was playing. I think he's the best player on the team. What did you do last night?

**Sheryl:** I watched a science fiction movie. It was very exciting.

**Brian:** I don't like science fiction. I think action films are more exciting.

**Sheryl:** Really?

> **Need help?**
>
> It was…
>   fantastic.
>   exciting.
>   interesting.
>   so-so.
>   not bad.
>   boring.

**C** Listen again and repeat.

**D** Work with a partner. Practice the conversation. Use the ideas in 1A or your own ideas.

**E** Listen to the 3 conversations. Complete the chart.

| Questions | Conversation 1 | Conversation 2 | Conversation 3 |
|---|---|---|---|
| What kinds of events are they talking about? A concert? A football game? A TV show? | a TV show | | |
| Did the man like it? Yes? No? | | | |
| Did the woman like it? Yes? No? | | | |

# 2 Use the comparative and superlative to express opinions

**A** What is your opinion about these sports? Write sentences with the superlative. Choose a different adjective from the box for each one.

| football | jogging | volleyball | basketball |

| healthy |
| relaxing |
| dangerous |
| exciting |
| boring |
| expensive |

*Football is the most exciting sport.*

1. _____
2. _____
3. _____

**B** Write sentences with the comparative. Choose sports from 2A or other sports you know.

*Football is more exciting than golf.*

1. _____
2. _____
3. _____

> **Grammar note**
>
> **Comparative and superlative**
>
> Use the comparative to talk about two things.
>
> Use the superlative to talk about three or more things.

# 3 Real-life math

**A** Read the information about science museum ticket prices. Answer the questions.

1. Angela, her husband, and their two children, ages 8 and 10, are at the museum on Sunday. Which is the cheapest ticket?
   a. Regular admission     b. Family Day ticket

2. Simon and his two children, ages 12 and 16, are at the museum on Sunday. Which is the cheapest ticket?
   a. Regular admission     b. Family Day ticket

**B** Which ticket is best for you and your family?

---

**Science Museum**

**Regular admission**
Adults:  $7.50
Seniors over 60:  $5.00
Children under 14:  $5.00

**Family Day ticket**
 (Sunday only)
Two adults and up to three
   children under 14:  $22.00

---

**TEST YOURSELF** ✔

Role-play a conversation about a movie or TV show. Partner A: Tell your partner about a movie or TV show you saw recently. Partner B: Ask your partner for his or her opinion of the movie or TV show. Then change roles.

## 1 Get ready to read

**A** **Read the definitions. Look at the picture.**

border: the line between two countries, states, cities, etc.
canyon: a deep valley, often with a river at the bottom
sight: a famous or interesting place
view: what you can see from a certain place

canyon

**B** **Look at the pictures. Think of one question to ask about each place.
Write the questions in your notebook.**

## 2 Read about places to visit in the U.S.

**A** **Read the article. Does it answer your questions?**

# Sights in the U.S.

**Washington, D.C.,** is the capital[1] of the United States. One important building in Washington, D.C., is the White House. It is at 1600 Pennsylvania Avenue. The president lives and works there. People can visit the White House. You need a group of ten or more people. You can write to your U.S. representative or senator for tickets.

**Niagara Falls** is on the border between the United States and Canada. They are the largest waterfalls in North America. More than 750,000 gallons of water go over the falls each second. A boat called the *Maid of the Mist* takes tourists to the bottom of the falls.

**The Grand Canyon** is a large national park in Arizona. It is one of the most amazing places in the world. The canyon is 277 miles long. Its natural beauty brings thousands of visitors to this park every year. Visitors can go hiking, camping, or bird watching. Or they can just stand and enjoy the view!

**The Golden Gate Bridge** is in San Francisco, a city on the West Coast of the United States. The bridge is the most famous sight in San Francisco. It opened in 1937 and is 1.7 miles long. From the bridge, pedestrians, cyclists, and cars can enjoy the view of the Pacific Ocean and San Francisco.

[1] capital: city where the government of a country or state is located

**B** Listen and read the article again.

**C** Mark the sentences T (true) or F (false).

   F   1. Visitors can go to the White House at any time.

_____ 2. The largest waterfalls in North America are the Niagara Falls.

_____ 3. The Grand Canyon National Park is in Arizona.

_____ 4. You can walk or drive across the Golden Gate Bridge.

_____ 5. You can see the Atlantic Ocean from the Golden Gate Bridge.

**D** Complete the sentences. Use the words in the box.

| sight | view | border | capital |
|-------|------|--------|---------|

1. Washington, D.C., is the _____ of the U.S.

2. You can get a good _____ of Niagara Falls from a boat.

3. Niagara Falls is on the _____ between the U.S. and Canada.

4. The Golden Gate Bridge is the most famous _____ in San Francisco.

## 3 Read a road map

**A** Look at the map and measure the distances. Answer the questions.

1. How far is it from Philadelphia to Washington, D.C.?

  _____

2. You are driving at about 60 miles per hour. How long will the trip take?

  _____

3. How many states will you drive through?

  _____

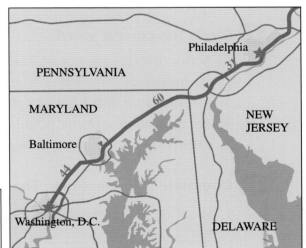

KEY

**44** = number of miles

1 inch = 48 miles

**B** Find a road map of your area. Choose 2 places and find the distance between them.

**BRING IT TO LIFE**

Find information on the Internet or in your community about 2 other places to visit in the U.S. What sights can you see at each place? Talk about the information with your class.

## 1 Grammar

**A** Write the superlative forms in the chart.

| Adjectives | Superlative | Adjectives | Superlative |
|---|---|---|---|
| funny | | good | |
| long | | scary | |
| expensive | | bad | |
| sad | | famous | |
| interesting | | cheap | |

**B** Correct the sentences. Add *the* or *than* to each sentence.

1. Niagara Falls is one of ^the^ most famous tourist sights in North America.

2. I think football is more exciting basketball.

3. Is bungee-jumping scarier diving?

4. Watching a DVD is cheaper going to the movies.

5. Camping is one of most popular types of vacation in the U.S.

**C** Circle the correct words.

1. Action movies are ( (more exciting) / the most exciting ) than romantic movies.
2. Swimming is ( more relaxing / the most relaxing ) than jogging.
3. I think baseball is ( better / the best ) than football.
4. Are quiz shows ( more popular / the most popular ) type of TV show?
5. I think diving is ( more dangerous / the most dangerous ) sport.

**D** Complete the questions. Then write your opinion. Use the superlative.

1. What is ___the most interesting___ type of movie? (interesting)

   _____

2. What is _____ city in the U.S.? (exciting)

   _____

3. What is _____ type of vacation? (cheap)

   _____

4. What is _____ way to travel? (comfortable)

   _____

# 2 Group work

**A** Work with 2–3 classmates. Write a paragraph of 8 sentences about your weekend plans. Talk about your plans with the class.

*On Saturday, my friend and I went to the movies. We saw the best action movie. Then…*

**B** Interview 3 classmates. Write their answers in the chart.

| What is… | Classmate 1 | Classmate 2 | Classmate 3 |
|---|---|---|---|
| the most exciting sport to watch? | | | |
| the most dangerous sport to play? | | | |
| the best music to dance to? | | | |
| the most boring type of movie? | | | |
| the best type of TV show? | | | |

**C** Talk about the answers with your class.

## PROBLEM SOLVING

**A** Listen and read about Tara's problem.

Tara's children like to watch TV for four or more hours every day. Tara thinks TV is OK, but only for an hour each day. She thinks that there are better things for her children to do. When she tells her children that they should do other things, they say, "TV is more interesting than that." When she turns off the TV, her children get angry. Tara is worried about her children, but she doesn't know what to do.

**B** Work with your classmates. Answer the questions.

1. What is Tara's problem?
2. What can she do? Think of 2 or 3 solutions to her problem.

## THE FIRST STEP  Let's get started

### Pg. 3  Let's get started—Exercise 5A

M = Man, W = Woman
W: Days of the week: Sunday, Monday, Tuesday,
Wednesday, Thursday, Friday, Saturday
M: Months of the year: January, February, March, April,
May, June, July, August, September, October,
November, December

## UNIT 1  Learning to Learn

### Pg. 4  Lesson 1—Exercise 1B

S = Sam, D = Dana, E = East Asian Male, L = Linda,
S1 = Student 1, S2 = Student 2, N = Naomi, F = Fernando,
F1 = Female Voice, M = Male voice, A = Ahmed

1. S: I like to copy new words in my notebook. I'm
learning about classroom language. Here are the
words I need to copy: *paper, pen,* and *pencil.*
2. D: Do you want to practice with me?
   E: Yes, I like to practice with a partner.
3. L: Let's brainstorm some words. We need words for
*write* and *read.* Say your ideas, and I'll write them
in this notebook.
   S1: Hmm, for *write: pen.*
   S2: Let's see. And for *read: book!*
   L: Good! I like to brainstorm words.
4. N: Great! It's my turn to use a computer. I learn so
much when I use a computer.
5. F: I need to look up this word. What is *chalk?* Oh,
I understand! I like to look up words in the
dictionary.
6. F1: What are you doing?
   M: I'm learning English.
   A: I like to listen to CDs. You can listen again and
again.

### Pg. 5  Lesson 1—Exercise 2B

S1 = Student 1, N = Narrator, S2 = Student 2,
S5 = Student 5, S3 = Student 3, S4 = Student 4,
S6 = Student 6, S7 = Student 7, S8 = Student 8,
RV = Recorded Voice, S9 = Student 9, S10 = Student 10

1. S1: OK, let's work with the flashcards. What's on
this flashcard?
   N: flashcards
2. S2: Hmmm. The word is *pen.* I like to work with a
partner.
   S1: Mmm-hmmm. Yes, pair work is good practice.
   N: pair
3. S5: Our group has three people in it. Is that OK?
   S4: Yes, that's fine.
   S3: Great!
   N: group
4. S3: This is my notebook. I write in my notebook
every day.
   N: notebook
5. S4: Here's a picture of a school. I like to draw
pictures.
   N: picture

6. S6: What's this word—*chalk?* I need my dictionary.
The dictionary says, chalk is usually white or
yellow. You use it to write on a blackboard. Oh,
yes, teachers use chalk.
   N: dictionary
7. S7: I'm making a chart. This chart will help me to
organize information.
   N: chart
8. S8: I think there's a problem with the CD player. Let
me see.
   RV: "He likes to study."
   S8: Aha! That's better!
   N: CD player
9. S9: This is the Internet.
   S10: I'm on the Internet?
   S9: Yes, this is the school's homepage.
   N: the Internet

### Pg. 7  Lesson 2—Exercise 3A

D = Dan, M = Min
D: Hey, Min. Can I see your vocabulary notebook?
M: Sure, Dan. Here it is.
D: Oh. You have a lot of pictures in here!
M: I like to draw pictures of new words. It helps me
remember the definitions.
D: I don't like to draw. I really like to see new words
and hear new words.
M: Yes, I like to see new words, and I like to hear them,
too. That helps with the pronunciation.
D: I always like to say new words two or three times.
M: Really? Maybe I need to do that. I always like to
write new words in sentences.
D: I do that too, and I also like to put new words in a
chart. I use different colors for the chart.
M: I don't use charts, but it sounds like a good idea.

### Pg. 10  Lesson 4—Exercise 1A

K = Kenji, H = Haruko, L = Ling, S = Mr. Singh,
M = Ms. Morgan, Z = Zoila, B = Barbara, C = Chanda,
A = Achir

1. K: Haruko, let me introduce my friend, Ling.
   H: Excuse me? What's your name?
   L: Ling. L-I-N-G.
   H: Nice to meet you, Ling.
   K: And you know me, I'm Kenji.
   H: Good, the introductions are over.
2. S: Zoila, I'd like to introduce our new teaching
assistant, Ms. Jane Morgan. Ms. Morgan, this is
Zoila Ramirez.
   M: Nice to meet you, Zoila. How do you spell your
first name?
   Z: Z-O-I-L-A.
   M: Oh, that's a nice name.
   Z: Thank you.
3. B: And who is this handsome young man, Chanda?
   C: Barbara, meet my grandson, Achir.
   B: What's your name again?
   A: Achir. A-C-H-I-R.
   B: Nice to meet you, Achir.

# UNIT 2    Getting Together

## Pg. 16  Lesson 1—Exercise 1B

W = Woman, D = Dan, M = Man, J = Jim, W2 = Woman 2,
T = Tara, F = Fernando, G = Gloria, R = Rob, M2 = Man 2
(on phone), P = Priya

1.  W:  What's the matter, Dan? You look bored.
    D:  It's raining, and I can't go out. I am bored.
2.  M:  Hey, Jim. You look frustrated.
    J:  I am! I'm late for work, and look at my car.
        Covered in snow! Help me get it out!
3.  W2: Tara, you look tired this morning.
    T:  Yes, it's so dark and cloudy. I'm sleepy.
4.  F:  Hi, Gloria. Isn't this a beautiful spring day?
    G:  Flowers? For me? Oh, Fernando! I'm so
        surprised!
5.  R:  What a beautiful, sunny day! I always feel
        cheerful on days like this.
6.  M2: What's the matter, Priya? You sound upset.
    P:  I am upset. You know that bad storm last night?
        You should see what it did. There's a tree on
        my car!

## Pg. 17  Lesson 1—Exercise 2B

M1 = Man, N = Narrator, W1 = Woman, M2 = Man 2,
W2 = Woman 2, M3 = Man 3, W3 = Woman 3,
W4 = Woman 4, M4 = Man 4

1.  M1: Wow, it's raining very hard. What a
        thunderstorm! Let's go inside.
    N:  thunderstorm
2.  W1: Oh, look at the lightning! Hey! Don't stand
        under the tree!
    N:  lightning
3.  M2: We had a bad snowstorm this weekend. The
        streets are full of snow.
    N:  snowstorm
4.  M2: Brrr. It's only 32 degrees outside today. It's
        freezing.
    N:  freezing
5.  W2: Watch out! The sidewalk is very icy.
    N:  icy
6.  M3: Where's my sweater? It's cool today.
    N:  cool
7.  W3: It's very foggy this morning. I can't see
        anything. It's hard to drive when it's so foggy.
    N:  foggy
8.  W4: Phew! It's very hot outside. The thermometer
        says 102 degrees.
    N:  hot
9.  M4: It's not just hot. It's humid, too. The air is heavy
        with 98 percent humidity. Ugh!
    N:  humid

## Pg. 19  Lesson 2—Exercise 3A

And now it's time for the community calendar. Summer
is a great time in our community. Here are some things
that are going on in July and August. There's a baseball
game at River Stadium on Wednesday evening, July 27th.
The game starts at 8 o'clock. Come and bring your
family. That's Wednesday, July 27th, at 8 p.m. at River
Stadium. Summer is also the season for music. As always,
there's the International Music Festival in Bridge Street
Park. This year the two-day festival is on July 30th and
31st. It starts at 11 o'clock in the morning both days.

That's at 11 a.m. in Bridge Street Park on July 30th and
31st. And finally, we want to see you all at the County
Fair. There will be good food and lots of exciting things
to see and do. The fair starts at 9 o'clock in the morning
on Saturday, August 6th, and Sunday, August 7th. That's
9 a.m. on August 6th and 7th. We'll see you there. Now
for today's…

## Pg. 22  Lesson 4—Exercise 1E

S = Sara, J = Jenny

S:  I'm having a party next Saturday afternoon at about 2
    o'clock. Would you like to come?
J:  Sure! I'd love to. How do I get there?
S:  It's easy. Take the train to the First Street Station. Go
    out of the train station and continue straight on First
    St. Go over the bridge and turn right on Grant Street.
    Go past Second Street and the bank. Take the next
    street on the left.
J:  Let's see if I understand. Go straight out of the train
    station. Then go over the bridge and turn right. Go
    past the bank and take Second Street on the left.
S:  No, go past Second Street. Turn left on the next
    street. The name of that street is Third Street.
J:  OK, go past Second Street and turn left onto Third
    Street. And your house is… ?
S:  Oh, yeah. My house is the third house on the right.
    It's a red house and the number is 238.
J:  Great, I'll see you on Saturday at 2 o'clock.

## Pg. 23  Lesson 4—Exercise 2C

W1 = Woman 1, M1 = Man 1, M2 = Man 2, M3 = Man 3,
W2 = Woman 2, W3 = Woman 3

1.  W1: Do I take the second street on the right?
    M1: No, take the first street on the right.
2.  M2: Do I go past the school?
    W1: No, go past the supermarket.
3.  W2: Do I go under the bridge?
    M1: No, go over the bridge.
4.  M3: Do I go around the supermarket?
    W3: No, go around the post office.

## Pg. 23  Lesson 4—Exercise 2D

W = Woman, M = Man

1.  W:  Do I take the second street on the right?
    M:  No, take the first street on the right.
2.  M:  Do I go past the school?
    W:  No, go past the supermarket.

# UNIT 3    Moving Out

## Pg. 28  Lesson 1—Exercise 1B

W = Woman, M = Man

1.  W:  This house has too many problems. For one
        thing, there's a dripping faucet in the bathroom.
    M:  Hey, it's an old house. I can fix a dripping faucet.
        That's easy.
2.  W:  There's a broken door in the bedroom.
    M:  Yes, I see that. Broken doors are no big deal. I'll
        call someone to fix it.
3.  W:  Look at this! Water! It's all over the floor in the
        kitchen.
    M:  Don't worry. It's just a leaking pipe under the
        kitchen sink. I can fix it.

4. W: EEEEK! Mice! There are mice in the garage! Get rid of them!
   M: No problem. We can call the exterminator in the morning.
5. M: Hey! Turn on the light, please. It's dark down here.
   W: I can't. There's no electricity in the basement.
   M: No electricity? What a house!
6. W: Here's one more thing. There's a cracked window in the living room.
   M: OK, OK. I agree. This house has a lot of problems.

## Pg. 29 Lesson 1—Exercise 2B

M = Man, N = Narrator, W = Woman
1. M: The repair person is fixing the broken window.
   N: repair person
2. W: The plumber is in the kitchen. He's fixing the pipe under the sink.
   N: plumber
3. M: The electrician is in the kitchen, too. There's no electricity.
   N: electrician
4. W: The electrician is checking the fuse box. Maybe that's the problem.
   N: fuse box
5. M: The carpenter is repairing the broken door in the bedroom.
   N: carpenter
6. M: The lock on the front door is broken.
   N: lock
7. W: The locksmith is replacing the lock.
   N: locksmith
8. W: There's the exterminator with a picture of a cockroach on his uniform. The exterminator is getting rid of the mice and cockroaches.
   N: exterminator
9. M: Ugh! I see a cockroach! Where's the exterminator?
   N: cockroach

## Pg. 31 Lesson 2—Exercise 3A

A = Anya, T = Teresa
A: Well, my dream home isn't in the housing ads today!
T: What are you looking for in a home, Anya?
A: Well, I really need three bedrooms. The boys are sharing a bedroom now. I think they need their own rooms.
T: So you want three bedrooms, and how many bathrooms?
A: We're fine with two bathrooms. That's all we need. One for Pavel and me, and one for the boys.
T: OK, two bathrooms. How about the location?
A: Well, for the kids, we need to be near the school.
T: Hmm, near the school. And how much do you want to pay for this dream home?
A: That's the problem. I can't pay a lot of rent. I need to find a home for $500 a month.
T: Wow, $500! That is a dream! But you never know. Let's look at the housing ads one more time. Maybe your dream home is there.
A: I hope you're right.

## Pg. 34 Lesson 4—Exercise 1E

S = Sharon, R = Mr. Reynolds, W1 = Woman 1,
W2 = Woman 2
1. S: Hello. My name is Sharon. Is Mr. Reynolds there?
   R: Yes, this is Mr. Reynolds.
   S: Hi. I'm calling about the apartment for rent on Maple Street. Can you give me some information?
   R: Yes, of course. What do you want to know?
   S: How much is the rent?
   R: It's $600 a month.
   S: OK. How much is the deposit?
   R: It's one month's rent.
   S: Hmm. That's another $600 for the deposit. Does it include utilities, for example, gas, heat, and hot water?
   R: No, it doesn't.
   S: When will the apartment be available?
   R: On January 1st.
   S: Can I come and look at it, please?
   R: Sure. How about tomorrow?
   S: Great. See you then.
2. S: Hello. I am calling about the apartment for rent at 15 Center Street. Can you give me some information?
   W1: Yes, of course.
   S: How much is the rent?
   W1: It's $750 a month.
   S: Is there a security deposit?
   W1: Yes. The security deposit is $500. Oh, and utilities are not included.
   S: OK, the utilities cost extra. When will the apartment be free?
   W1: On December 15th.
   S: Can I come and look at it, please?
   W1: Well, I'm busy today. How about tomorrow morning?
   S: That would be fine.
3. S: Hello. I am calling about the apartment on Second Avenue. I need more information.
   W2: What do you want to know?
   S: Well, how much is the rent?
   W2: It's $1200 a month.
   S: Is there a deposit?
   W2: Yes, the deposit is $600.
   S: That's not very much. What about the utilities?
   W2: Yes, the monthly rent includes utilities.
   S: Oh, good. When will the apartment be available?
   W2: On January 1st.
   S: Can I come and look at it, please?
   W2: When do you want to see it?
   S: Could I come this afternoon?
   W2: Sure! How about three o'clock?
   S: See you at 3:00.

# UNIT 4  Looking for Work

## Pg. 40  Lesson 1—Exercise 1B

1. This is Katia Sousa, and she's filling out a job application. She writes her name, address, and telephone number in the personal information section.
2. Then she completes the job skills section. She can use computers. So she checks "yes" for that question. She can also speak English and Portuguese very well.
3. Next she fills in the information about her education. She went to County Community College in Tampa for two years and graduated in 2006.
4. Next she fills out her employment history. She's working at Sam's Supermarket now, so she writes that job in first.
5. In the references section, Katia writes the names of her boss at the supermarket, Sam Giannini, and of a teacher from her college, Beth Marcello.

## Pg. 41  Lesson 1—Exercise 2B

W = Woman, N = Narrator, M = Man, W2 = Job counselor, M2 = Mr. Young

1. W:  This is a Job Center. The woman standing behind the table helps people find jobs. She is a job counselor.
   N:  job counselor
2. M:  The man sitting at the table is Mr. Young. He's looking for a job. He is a job applicant.
   N:  job applicant
3. W:  The job counselor is telling Mr. Young about different jobs.
   W2:  An accountant works with money and helps people with their taxes. You have strong math skills. You could be an accountant.
   N:  accountant
4. W2:  Mail carriers deliver mail to homes and businesses. You work outside a lot when you are a mail carrier.
   N:  mail carrier
5. W2:  A mover brings furniture to a new home. Do you like physical work? Maybe you could be a mover.
   N:  mover
6. W2:  Veterinarians take care of sick animals. Do you want to be an animal doctor? Then think about a career as a veterinarian.
   N:  veterinarian
7. W2:  A chef works in a restaurant kitchen. Chefs cook the food. Do you like to cook? Think about a career as a chef.
   N:  chef
8. W2:  A sales clerk has an interesting job. A sales clerk helps customers in a store and meets lots of people. Maybe you can be a sales clerk.
   N:  sales clerk
9. W2:  And finally, you could think about a job as a computer programmer. A computer programmer writes and tests new programs for computers.
   N:  computer programmer
   W2:  Well, what do you think, Mr. Young?
   M2:  I think I want to be a job counselor.

## Pg. 43  Lesson 2—Exercise 3A

R = Rick, A = Alexa
R:  Alexa, did you see these jobs in the paper? Maybe one of them is good for you.
A:  Well, I saw the job for a chef. That looks quite good. But it's only part-time, and written references are required. I don't have any references.
R:  Maybe you could call Bob at the restaurant where you worked. You could ask him for a reference.
A:  Yes, that's true. But what about this other job as a sales clerk at the Mobile Phone Center? It says you need to be good at talking to people. I can do that!
R:  Yes, but do you know anything about phones?
A:  No, but I can learn!
R:  Well, that job might be better for you. It's full-time, and you don't need any references. Why don't you give them a call?
A:  I think I'll call right now.

## Pg. 46  Lesson 4—Exercise 1E

I1 = Interviewer 1, J1 = Job applicant 1,
I2 = Interviewer 2, J2 = Job applicant 2,
I3 = Interviewer 3, J3 = Job applicant 3

1. I1:  Now, let's see. What did you do in your last job?
   J1:  Well, I was an assistant manager at a supermarket.
   I1:  That's good. Did you work with computers?
   J1:  Yes, I did. I took the money from the cashiers at the end of the day. I had to count it and enter the amounts in the computer.
   I1:  Ah, so you're good at math.
   J1:  Oh, yes. That's why I decided to study accounting.
2. I2:  Do you have any experience talking with customers?
   J2:  Yes, I talked with customers a lot in my job at ABC Rentals.
   I2:  Do you know a lot about cars?
   J2:  Yes, I do! I was a mechanic at Tom's Garage for three years.
   I2:  OK. That sounds very good.
3. I3:  Could you tell me about your job skills?
   J3:  I'm very careful, and I'm never late for work.
   I3:  What did you do in your last job?
   J3:  I worked in the mail room at a factory.
   I3:  OK. Do you like to walk a lot?
   J3:  Yes, that's no problem. It's great exercise. I like to talk to people, too. And I love dogs!

# UNIT 5  On the Job

## Pg. 52  Lesson 1—Exercise 1B

1. Hmm, there's a lot of information on this pay stub. Let's see if it's all correct. Here's the pay period. It's for seven days. And there's my name, Pablo Ramirez.
2. OK, I see the number of hours I worked, 28 hours. And my hourly rate is $15.25. That's right, I get paid $15.25 per hour.
3. So, 28 hours times $15.25 is $427. I earned a total of $427. That's my gross pay.

4. Now, what about the deductions? That is the money that my employer takes out of my gross pay. Wow! The deductions for this pay period are $93!
5. After taking out all the deductions, my net pay is $334. That's the money I take home!
6. Now, let's see. How much did I pay in taxes this month? The deduction for state tax is $19.10. For federal tax, it's $42.70.
7. The deduction for Medicare is $6.20.
8. And last but not least, I paid $25 for Social Security. Well, Medicare and Social Security will help me when I'm older. So I guess it's a good thing.

### Pg. 53 Lesson 1—Exercise 2B

W = Woman, N = Narrator
W: This is our office at the factory. It can be a very busy place. There are a lot of office machines and other things in here, so please be careful!
1. W: The fax machine is on the desk next to the computer, on the left. We can also use the fax machine to make phone calls.
   N: fax machine
2. W: The computer is on the desk, in the center. We use the computer for many different jobs at the factory.
   N: computer
3. W: The fax machine, the computer, and the printer are all on the desk. The printer is to the right of the computer. We use it to print letters and other documents.
   N: printer
4. W: The scanner is on a small table next to the desk, on the right. The office assistant is going to scan those photographs.
   N: scanner
5. W: The photocopier is that big machine next to the woman with the yellow shirt. She is copying some documents now.
   N: photocopier
6. W: The file cabinet is next to the photocopier. We keep our important papers there.
   N: file cabinet
7. W: The time clock is on the wall near the door. There's a card for every employee under the time clock. All of the employees have to punch the time clock every day. This way, the manager knows exactly what time the employees are at work.
   N: time clock
8. W: The vending machine is also near the door. Employees can buy food and drinks from the vending machine.
   N: vending machine
9. W: In the Deliveries area of the Mills Brothers factory, a man is operating a forklift. He's using the forklift to move some big boxes.
   N: forklift

### Pg. 55 Lesson 2—Exercise 3A

M = Manager, J = Jim
M: Hi, Jim. Welcome to Mills Brothers. I'm glad to see you're on time for work.

J: I don't like to be late, especially on my first day. Oh, and by the way, could you tell me, is there a company dress code?
M: Well, you have to wear appropriate clothing. No sandals or shorts. And, of course, you have to follow the safety rules.
J: I always do.
M: That's great. If you need anything, just ask for help. Have a good day.
J: Thanks. You too.

### Pg. 58 Lesson 4—Exercise 1E

M = Man, J = Jung-ju, W1 = Woman 1, R = Ruth,
W2 = Woman 2, S = Simon
1. M: Jung-ju, could you come over here for a minute?
   J: Yes, of course.
   M: Could you write an email for me, please? It has to be done right away.
   J: Yes, no problem. Do you need anything else?
   M: No, that's all for now.
2. W1: Ruth, could you help me?
   R: Yes, what is it?
   W1: Could you send a letter to Mr. Moya for me when you go out for lunch?
   R: Sure! No problem.
   W1: I just don't have time to do it myself.
   R: It's no trouble.
3. W2: Simon, did you make those copies for me?
   S: Yes, I did.
   W2: Where are the photocopies?
   S: They're on my desk.
   W2: Could you put them in the file cabinet, please?
   S: Yes, absolutely!

## UNIT 6   Pick up the Phone

### Pg. 64 Lesson 1—Exercise 1B

1. Here's my phone bill for this month. How much do I need to pay? $45.63? Oh, no. The previous charges for last month were $45.63. I paid that in April.
2. And for calls in this area? Oh, yes that's local service. It's $26.
3. So how much do I have to pay this month? Let's see...$26, and then $13.95 for long distance service. Here it is. The total due is $39.95. Well, that's not too bad!
4. OK, now let me look at page two for the long distance calls this month.
5. Hmm, right, I made two domestic calls. One was to my parents in Florida, and one was to my sister in Texas. How much were they? $1.80 and $1.65. So, my domestic calls total $3.45.
6. And here are the international calls. One was to my aunt in Brazil, and one was to my friend in China. That's $6.00 and $4.50 for a total of $10.50.

### Pg. 65 Lesson 1—Exercise 2B

M = Man, N = Narrator, O1 = Operator 1, O2 = Operator 2,
N1 = Nadine, W = Woman, A = Answering machine
1. M: There's a fire in Nadine's kitchen. She's using her cordless phone to call for help. You can talk outside on a cordless phone.
   N: cordless phone

2. O1: 911. What's your emergency?

N1: There's a fire in my kitchen!

M: Nadine is calling emergency services to report the fire.

N: call emergency services

3. W: Kevin is in his office. He is using an answering machine. He has one new message.

N: answering machine

4. A: You have one new message.

W: Kevin is listening to a message on the answering machine.

N: listen to a message

5. M: Jim is using a cell phone. He can make telephone calls from the street with a cell phone.

N: cell phone

6. O2: Information. What city, please?

M: Jim needs the phone number for Tom's Restaurant. He's calling directory assistance.

N: call directory assistance

7. W: Carla doesn't have a cell phone. She is using a pay phone to call a taxi.

N: pay phone

8. W: Carla's at the supermarket in New City. She needs a taxi. She's calling a taxi on the pay phone.

N: call a taxi

## Pg. 67   Lesson 2—Exercise 3A

W1 = Woman 1, M1 = Man 1, W2 = Woman 2,
M2 = Man 2, W3 = Woman 3, M3 = Man 3,
M4 = Man 4, W4 = Woman 4, W5 = Woman 5,
M5 = Man 5, M6 = Man 6, W6 = Woman 6

1. W1: I can't come to class today.

M1: Are you sick?

W1: Yes, I am. I have a fever. I feel terrible.

M1: That's too bad. Stay home until you feel better.

W1: Thank you. Goodbye.

2. M2: I won't be at work today.

W2: What's the matter?

M2: I need to help my friend move. Can I take a sick day?

W2: Of course not. You aren't sick! You need to come to work.

M2: OK. I'll be there soon.

3. W3: Who are you calling?

M3: I'm calling my boss. I'm calling in sick.

W3: What's the matter?

M3: Well, I'm not really sick. I'm just a little tired today.

W3: A little tired! You can't call in sick for that!

M3: Yeah, I guess you're right.

4. M4: I can't come to work today.

W4: Why not? Is there a problem?

M4: My son is sick. I have to stay home with him today.

W4: OK. Well I hope he feels better then.

M4: Thanks. Have a good day.

5. W5: I need to stay home sick today. I have a bad cold.

M5: I'm sorry to hear that. Make sure you rest and drink plenty of water.

W5: Yes, I will.

M5: OK, I hope you feel better soon.

6. M6: I'm not coming to work today. I missed the bus this morning.

W6: Isn't there another bus?

M6: Yes, but I'll be very late.

W6: That's not a problem. You can work late this evening.

## Pg. 70   Lesson 4—Exercise 1E

J = Jack, W = Woman, H = Hal, L = Lois, S = Mrs. Smith,
M = Maria

1. J: Hello. May I speak to Mr. Reed, please?

W: He's not here right now. Can I take a message?

J: This is Jack Brown. I'm the new office assistant. I'm going to be late today.

W: Oh, what's the problem?

J: I have a problem with my car. I need to take it to the garage.

W: OK. What time will you be in?

J: I'll be in at 10:00.

W: I'll tell him. Thanks for calling. Bye.

J: Goodbye.

2. H: Hi, this is Hal Freeman. I'm one of the truck drivers. Can I speak to the manager, please?

L: Oh, hi Hal. This is Lois. I'm sorry, the manager's out right now.

H: Can I leave a message?

L: Of course.

H: I'm calling in sick today.

L: Oh, what's the matter?

H: I was lifting some heavy boxes yesterday, and I injured my back. Now I have a backache.

L: OK, I'll give the manager your message. Take care of yourself.

H: Thanks. I should be in tomorrow.

3. S: Central College. Can I help you?

M: Is Mrs. Smith there, please?

S: Yes, this is Mrs. Smith.

M: Can I leave a message for Mr. Green, please?

S: Yes, of course. Who's speaking, please?

M: This is Maria Ruiz. I'm an ESL student. I have a cold, and I can't come to class today.

S: I hope you feel better soon. I'll make sure Mr. Green gets your message.

M: Thanks a lot. Goodbye.

## Pg. 71   Lesson 4—Exercise 2B

M = Man, W = Woman

1. M: I want to live in Miami.
2. W: Where is his work?
3. M: How do you feel today?
4. W: I think we'll have to call the office.

# UNIT 7   What's for Dinner?

## Pg. 76   Lesson 1—Exercise 1B

1. Well! That's the groceries for this week, anyway! I should look at the receipt to check if I have everything. OK, here is the box of spaghetti. It cost only 79 cents.
2. The jar of peanut of butter was $2.69.
3. The can of tomato soup cost 99 cents.
4. There's the carton of milk. That was $1.29.
5. There's the package of cookies for $2.59.
6. Hmm, the bottle of oil cost $5.99.

7. And finally, the bag of potato chips was $1.99.
8. Oh, I almost forgot the bunch of bananas for $1.59. Now, I just have to put all this food away.

### Pg. 77 Lesson 1—Exercise 2B

W = Woman, N = Narrator, M = Man
1. W: Here on the kitchen counter we have many ingredients. In this bag, we have two pounds of flour.
   N: two pounds of flour
2. M: Well, we don't need two pounds for the recipe. We only need one cup of flour.
   N: one cup of flour
3. W: We also have plenty of milk. In this carton, we have one quart of milk.
   N: one quart of milk
4. M: Let's see. There's one pint of milk in this measuring cup. That's 2 cups of milk.
   N: one pint of milk
5. W: Here's the salt. For the recipe, we only need one teaspoon of salt.
   N: one teaspoon of salt
6. M: Hmm, here's a gallon of water. I think I will drink some water.
   N: one gallon of water
7. W: Where's the bag of sugar? We need one tablespoon of sugar, and then the recipe is finished.
   N: one tablespoon of sugar
8. M: Do we have any oil? Oh, there's the bottle. Hmm, there are twelve ounces of oil in this bottle.
   N: twelve ounces of oil

### Pg. 79 Lesson 2—Exercise 3A

K = Mrs. Kim, W = Mrs. Kim's friend
K: Oh, I need a jar of jam.
W: How about this 8-ounce jar of jam? It's $1.60.
K: But this jar is bigger and only costs $3.60. Isn't it cheaper?
W: No, the 12-ounce jar is more expensive. Look at the unit-price label. It's 30¢ an ounce, but the 8-ounce jar costs only 20¢ per ounce.
K: Oh, you're right. The 8-ounce jar is a better buy. I'll buy that one.

### Pg. 82 Lesson 4—Exercise 1E

C1 = Customer 1, E = Store employee, C2 = Customer 2, C3 = Customer 3
1. C1: Excuse me. Where are the eggs?
   E: They're in the dairy section, next to the butter.
   C1: OK. Thank you very much.
   E: You're very welcome!
2. C2: Excuse me. Could you tell me where the jam is?
   E: Yes, of course. Jam is in aisle 2, next to the canned soup.
   C2: Thanks!
   E: No problem.
3. E: Can I help you find anything?
   C3: Yes, please. Can you tell me where the sausages are?
   E: Of course. They're in the meat section. We have pork, beef, and vegetarian sausages.
   C3: That's great! Thanks a lot!

### Pg. 83 Lesson 4—Exercise 2B

M = Man, W = Woman
| M: | grape | grapes |
| W: | orange | oranges |
| M: | sausage | sausages |
| W: | lunch | lunches |
| M: | jar | jars |
| W: | bunch | bunches |
| M: | mushroom | mushrooms |
| W: | carton | cartons |

## UNIT 8  Stay Safe and Well

### Pg. 88 Lesson 1—Exercise 1B

W1 = Woman 1, M1 = Man 1, D = Darla, T = Tom, W2 = Woman 2, M2 = Man 2, J = Jane
1. W1: Ouch! Oh no, I cut my finger.
   M1: Wash it off, and I'll get the antibiotic ointment.
2. M1: This heartburn is killing me!
   W1: Hold on. I think I have antacid in my bag.
3. D: Are you all right, Tom?
   T: No, I think I need some cough syrup.
4. W1: How's your earache doing?
   W2: Pretty good, thanks. I'm using eardrops, and they're working quite well.
5. M1: Allergies again?
   M2: Yes, I'm taking some antihistamine, but it doesn't work very well.
6. M1: What's up, Jane? You don't look so good.
   J: Do you have any pain reliever at your desk? I have a terrible headache.
   M1: Just a minute. I'll take a look.

### Pg. 89 Lesson 1—Exercise 2B

1. Gina has the measles. She has a rash on her face.
   have a rash
2. Olivia has a bad headache. Sometimes when you have the flu, you can have a headache.
   have a headache
3. Olivia also feels very hot. She has a fever.
   have a fever
4. Carlos is allergic to flowers. He sneezes all the time in the spring.
   sneeze
5. Van has a bad cold. With her cold, she has a cough.
   have a cough
6. Van also has a runny nose with her cold. You use a lot of tissues when you have a runny nose.
   have a runny nose
7. Abdul needs to sit down. He is dizzy.
   be dizzy
8. Abdul also feels sick to his stomach. He is nauseous.
   be nauseous
9. Jiang has a sprained ankle. His ankle is very swollen.
   be swollen

### Pg. 91 Lesson 2—Exercise 3A

M1 = Man 1, W1 = Woman 1, W2 = Woman 2, M2 = Man 2, W3 = Woman 3, W4 = Woman 4
1. M1: Hello. I need to make an appointment with Dr. Briggs.
   W1: What's the problem?

M1: I have a bad toothache. When can I see the doctor?

W1: Can you come in at 8 a.m. next Tuesday?

M1: Do you have any appointments before that?

W1: Well, let's see. How about at 11 a.m. this Friday?

M1: That's better.

W1: Can you give me your name?

M1: Of course, it's Simon Jackson.

W1: Mr. Jackson, your appointment is with Dr. Briggs at 11 a.m. on Friday, July 23rd. OK?

M1: Yes, that's fine. Thank you.

2. W2: Good morning, Dr. Richmond's office.

M2: Can I make an appointment, please?

W2: Yes, of course. Why do you need to see the doctor?

M2: I have a backache. The pain is in my lower back.

W2: OK. How about 3:45 this Thursday afternoon?

M2: That's great.

W2: What is your name, please?

M2: It's Ed Smith.

W2: OK, Mr. Smith. Then we'll see you at 3:45 p.m. on Thursday, November 15th.

M2: Thanks a lot.

3. W3: Hi, could I make an appointment with Dr. Garcia, please?

W4: Yes, of course. What's the appointment for?

W3: My two-year-old son has a stomachache.

W4: We have an appointment tomorrow. That's Wednesday, April 6th, at 10:00 o'clock in the morning.

W3: Do you have anything today?

W4: Hmm. How about 1 o'clock this afternoon?

W3: That's fine.

W4: Could I have your names, please?

W3: Yes, my name is Molly Brown, and my son's name is Peter.

W4: OK. We'll see you and your son at 1:00 p.m. this afternoon, Tuesday, April 5th.

W3: Thank you very much. Goodbye.

## Pg. 94 Lesson 4—Exercise 1E

P1 = Pharmacist 1, C1 = Customer 1, C2 = Customer 2, P2 = Pharmacist 2, P3 = Pharmacist 3, C3 = Customer 3

1. P1: 24-hour Pharmacy. Can I help you?

C1: Yes. Could you refill my prescription, please?

P1: What's your prescription number?

C1: 6-9-7-4-5-5.

P1: OK. That's 6-9-7-4-5-4.

C1: No, no. It's 6-9-7-4-5-5.

P1: Oh. OK, I found it. Luis Tarmin, right?

C1: Yes, that's it.

P1: Oh, wait a minute. I'm sorry. Your prescription expired on October 23rd, 2006. You need to see your doctor for a new prescription.

C1: Really? I'll call my doctor then. Thanks a lot.

2. C2: Could you fill this prescription for me, please?

P2: Yes, of course. What's your prescription number?

C2: My prescription number is 8-9-5-3-2-8.

P2: Is your last name Dawson?

C2: Yes, that's right. Lin Dawson.

P2: You need to take one pill every eight hours. Oh, and don't take more than three pills a day.

C2: OK. Can you tell me how many refills I have?

P2: You have two refills before February 28, 2008.

3. P3: Good morning. Can I help you?

C3: Yes. I'd like to refill my prescription, please.

P3: Last name, please?

C3: Ali. A-L-I. My first name is Fatima.

P3: Do you have your prescription number?

C3: Yes, it's 6-9-2-4-9-3.

P3: OK. Take one pill twice a day, one with breakfast and one with dinner. It will take me about 20 minutes to prepare this prescription. Can you wait?

C3: That's OK. I'll do some shopping and come back in about an hour.

# UNIT 9    Money Matters

## Pg. 100 Lesson 1—Exercise 1B

1. Let's see. I need to check my accounts. Where's my bank statement? Oh, here it is.
2. OK, I'm looking for the information about my checking account. Yes, it's right here on the statement.
3. It says my current balance is $850.
4. Yes, I wrote a personal check for $350.96 when I went to Green's Garden Store about two weeks ago.
5. How much cash do I have in my wallet? $21.
6. Oh, I remember. I used my ATM card yesterday and withdrew $40 from the bank.
7. How much is my credit card bill this month? Oh, yes. It's $540.
8. I'll have to withdraw money from my savings account. There's $1,800 in there…

## Pg. 101 Lesson 1—Exercise 2B

M = Man, N = Narrator

1. M: I'm using my ATM card for the first time. It says, "Insert your ATM card for service." OK, I put the card in here.

N: Insert your ATM card for service.

2. M: Now it says, "Enter your PIN." Hmm. Yes, I remember the number, it's…(fade)

N: Enter your PIN.

3. M: I need to insert the deposit envelope now. Where do I put the envelope?

N: Insert the deposit envelope now.

4. M: Now I want to take out some money. It says, "Enter the amount." OK. That's $40.00.

N: Enter the amount.

5. M: "Take your cash." Where's the money? Oh, here it is.

N: Take your cash.

6. M: Now I have to remove my card, and I'm done. That was easy.

N: Remove your card.

## Pg. 103 Lesson 2—Exercise 3A

It's time to fix up my living room. Let's see, what do I need? I might have some paint left from the kitchen, but I really need to buy some more paint. Hmm, I need a new table lamp and a new area rug. And I really need a new armchair, too. Wow! That's a lot. My total budget is about $400. Well, I could spend $30 on the paint. A new table lamp will cost about $40. And maybe I can get a discount on the area rug. It might cost only $150. How much do I have left for the armchair?

### Pg. 106 Lesson 4—Exercise 1E

Cu1 = Customer 1, Cl1 = Clerk 1, Cl2 = Clerk 2,
Cu2 = Customer 2, Cu3 = Customer 3, Cl3 = Clerk 3

1. Cu1: Excuse me. I'd like to return this sweater.
   Cl1: Why do you want to return it?
   Cu1: Because it doesn't fit. I really need a bigger one.
   Cl1: OK. Do you have your receipt?
   Cu1: Yes, here it is.
   Cl1: Do you want to choose something else?
   Cu1: No. Could I get a refund, please?
   Cl1: Yes, of course. That's no problem.
2. Cl2: Can I help you?
   Cu2: Yes, I need to return these socks, please.
   Cl2: Why are you returning them?
   Cu2: They're the wrong color.
   Cl2: Do you have your receipt?
   Cu2: I'm sorry. I don't.
   Cl2: We don't give refunds without a receipt, but you can exchange the socks for another pair.
   Cu2: OK. I'll do that.
3. Cu3: Hello. I would like to return this tie.
   Cl3: Is there a problem with it?
   Cu3: No, it's fine. I just don't wear ties.
   Cl3: OK. Can I have the receipt, please?
   Cu3: I don't have the receipt. My grandmother bought the tie for me.
   Cl3: I'm sorry, but if you don't have the receipt, you need to exchange the tie for another item.
   Cu3: Oh, well. I guess I have to exchange it.

### Pg. 107 Lesson 4—Exercise 2C

1. I'd like to return this ladder, please.
2. I like that red tie.
3. I have an ATM card, but I'd like a credit card, too.
4. I'd like to withdraw some cash from my checking account.
5. I like to shop at the home improvement store.
6. I'd like to fix up my kitchen.

## UNIT 10 Steps to Citizenship

### Pg. 112 Lesson 1—Exercise 1B

1. These are some of the citizenship requirements. You must be at least 18 years old. You also have to live in the United States for five or more years. Here are the other things I had to do.
2. I got my resident card in May 2001.
3. After five years, I filled out the Application for Naturalization and applied for citizenship. That was in June 2006.
4. I waited about one year. Then I had to take the citizenship test in May 2007.
5. Then I had to go to a special ceremony and take the oath of allegiance. I'll never forget that day. It was on July 18, 2007. I was very happy that I was finally a citizen of the United States.
6. Finally, on October 25, 2007, I got my U.S. passport.

### Pg. 113 Lesson 1—Exercise 2B

M = Man, N = Narrator, W = Woman
1. M: The president is the leader of the federal government.
   N: president

2. W: The vice president helps the president.
   N: vice president
3. M: A U.S. representative is a part of the House of Representatives. There are more than 400 U.S. representatives in the House of Representatives. They come from every part of the United States.
   N: U.S. representative
4. W: A U.S. senator is a part of the Senate. There are 100 U.S. senators in the Senate. Each state elects two U.S. senators.
   N: U.S. senator
5. M: The representatives and senators are in Congress.
   N: Congress
6. W: The governor is the leader of the state government.
   N: governor
7. M: The federal government has a vice president, but every state government has a lieutenant governor.
   N: lieutenant governor
8. W: A mayor is the leader of the local city government.
   N: mayor
9. M: The mayor works with the city council to make local laws.
   N: city council

### Pg. 115 Lesson 2—Exercise 3A

And now for some news from the Hillside High School Parent-Teacher Association. The Hillside High School PTA invites all parents to come to an Open House on October 10th, from 7 p.m. to 9 p.m. Meet the teachers and meet other parents, too. Snacks will be provided. Call Mr. Wu at 555-9401 for more information.

Help clean up our school! Join the Parent-Student Action Meeting on November 3rd. Bring cleaning supplies and tools. A sandwich lunch will be provided for everyone. Be there from 8 a.m. to 2 p.m. Call Mr. Perez at 555-6049 for more information.

See a student art show! On November 12th, we are holding our 5th annual student art show to raise money for school books. Come and support our students and your local community. The show is from 10:30 a.m. to 5 p.m. Call Mrs. Mason at 555-3989.

### Pg. 118 Lesson 4—Exercise 1E

O1 = Officer 1, D1 = Driver 1, O2 = Officer 2,
D2 = Driver 2, O3 = Officer 3, D3 = Driver 3

1. O1: Good afternoon. I need to see your driver's license and registration, please.
   D1: Of course. Here they are.
   O1: Do you know why I pulled you over?
   D1: No, I'm sorry, but I don't.
   O1: You were speeding. You were going 45 miles per hour in a 20-mile school zone. That's a $90 fine.
   D1: Wow! I'll be more careful next time.
2 . O2: Excuse me, sir. Can you give me your driver's license, please?
   D2: Sure. Here it is. What's the problem?
   O2: Your passenger is not wearing a seat belt. That's a traffic violation in this state.
   D2: I'm sorry. I didn't know that my passenger didn't have his seat belt on.

O2: Well, I'll let you go with a warning this time, but put your seat belt on right away.
3. O3: Driver's license, please.
   D3: Yes, sir. Here it is.
   O3: You didn't stop at that sign back there.
   D3: Oh, I'm sorry. I didn't see it.
   O3: That's too bad. But I still have to give you a ticket.

# UNIT 11 Deal with Difficulties

## Pg. 124 Lesson 1—Exercise 1B

M1 = Man 1, W1 = Woman 1, M2 = Man 2,
W2 = Woman 2, M3 = Man 3
1. M1: Did you hear about the robbery at the store yesterday? The robbers stole $500!
2. W1: There was a car accident this morning. Some cars crashed, but no one was hurt. Later, the traffic was terrible.
3. M2: There was a mugging in front of the bank yesterday. A man was walking past the bank when someone hit him and took his laptop.
4. W1: Where were you during the blackout?
   M2: I was on the subway!
5. W2: Did you hear about the gas explosion at the factory last night? Eight people were hurt.
6. M3: There's some vandalism in my neighborhood. Look at the building on the corner of Park Street and Third Avenue! Terrible! The windows are broken, and there's writing all over the walls!

## Pg. 125 Lesson 1—Exercise 2B

M1 = Man 1, N = Narrator, W1 = Woman 1,
W2 = Woman 2, W3 = Woman 3, M2 = Man 2,
M3 = Man 3, W4 = Woman 4, M4 = Man 4
1. M1: There was a lot of fire and smoke coming out of the volcano. It was a big volcanic eruption.
   N: volcanic eruption
2. W1: The sky was dark green, and it was very windy. Then we saw the tornado from miles away. We immediately went into the basement for protection from the tornado.
   N: tornado
3. W2: Last spring, there was a bad flood. The road in front of our house was completely under water from the flood.
   N: flood
4. W3: We had a heavy snowstorm, and it was very windy. In one day, we got 15 inches of snow! I will never forget that blizzard.
   N: blizzard
5. M2: There was a very strong wind and a lot of rain. It was the worst hurricane of the season.
   N: hurricane
6. M3: We had no rain for over six months. The river dried up, and there wasn't enough water for the plants during the drought.
   N: drought
7. W4: The trees in the forest near our house caught on fire. We called the firefighters, and they came to fight the forest fire.
   N: forest fire

8. M4: The earth was moving, and all of the buildings were shaking. It was a very strong earthquake.
   N: earthquake

## Pg. 127 Lesson 2—Exercise 3A

M1 = Man 1, W1 = Woman 1, W2 = Woman 2,
M2 = Man 2
1. M1: Did you hear about Al?
   W1: No. What happened to him?
   M1: He saw a car accident.
   W1: Where was the accident?
   M1: At the corner of 34th and West Street. Right outside his home.
   W1: What did he do?
   M1: He called the police.
   W1: Was anyone hurt?
   M1: I don't think so.
2. W1: Did you hear about Parvin?
   W2: No. What happened to her?
   W1: She saw a mugging.
   W2: Where did the mugging happen?
   W1: In the subway station.
   W2: What did she do?
   W1: She used her cell phone to call 911.
   W2: Was anyone hurt?
   W1: I think everyone was OK, but Parvin was really upset.
3. M1: Did you hear about Ella?
   M2: No. What happened to her?
   M1: There was a robbery when she was on vacation.
   M2: Oh no! At her home?
   M1: Yes, that's right. At 238 Westside Avenue.
   M2: What did she do?
   M1: She called the police, but they couldn't do much.
   M2: Did they take a lot?
   M1: I'm not sure. I think maybe just the TV and her computer.
   M2: Oh, not her computer! She's probably very upset.

## Pg. 130 Lesson 4—Exercise 1A

When you dial 911, the operator will ask you, "What is your emergency?" You must say if it is a fire, a medical emergency, or a police emergency. It is very important to know what is an emergency, and what isn't an emergency. For example, you can go to the police if someone takes your bicycle, but you don't call 911. You do call 911 if you see a robbery in your neighbor's home. If you see or smell smoke or see any kind of fire, you should call 911. Some people call the fire department when their cat runs up a tree, but that's not an emergency! If you have a small cut or burn on your finger, you can go to the doctor, but you don't need an ambulance. But if someone has a broken leg, that's serious. That's when you call 911.

## Pg. 130 Lesson 4—Exercise 1E

O = Operator, W = Woman, M = Man
1. O: 911. What is your emergency?
   W: It's a police emergency.
   O: Where are you?
   W: I'm at home. My address is 4230 Greentree Avenue.

O: What happened?
W: Someone is downstairs. I heard the window breaking.

2. O: 911. What is your emergency?
M: There's a fire.
O: Where are you?
M: I'm walking down South Street.
O: Where is the fire?
M: It's in the street. I can see smoke coming out of the window of a car.
O: OK, the firefighters are on their way. What's your name please?

## UNIT 12 Take the Day Off

### Pg. 136 Lesson 1—Exercise 1B

1. My family loves outdoor activities. We do all kinds of sports and outdoor activities at different times of the year.
Here's a picture of the children hiking in April. Gabriela and Marcos like to go hiking in the spring.

2. And this is our backyard. My husband Pedro and the children are playing softball. Every May, they play softball for hours.

3. Oh, I remember that day at the beach in August. It was really hot, and we went biking! Pedro just had to go biking that day!

4. I took this picture when the boys went fishing in September. They caught a really big fish that day! I don't really like to go fishing, but Pedro and Marcos love it!

5. Here's Pedro trying to light a campfire when we went camping last October. He worked for hours making that campfire! He said, "When people go camping, they need a campfire!"

6. And look! Here's a picture of my daughter and me. We went skating on the pond near our house last December. We always go skating in the winter. Wow, now that I think about it, our family is very active!

### Pg. 137 Lesson 1—Exercise 2B

M = Man, N = Narrator

1. M: We have many computer programs for all of our customers. If you like games, look at our great selection and choose a computer game.
N: computer game

2. M: Do you like fast and exciting computer games? No problem! We have the best action games in town. Try *Danger Team*, our newest action game.
N: action

3. M: We also have educational computer programs. In the educational section, you'll find a variety of programs for learning foreign languages, for example, the computer program *Portuguese in 10 Lessons.*
N: educational

4. M: We have many DVDs, too. All the newest and most popular movies are on DVD. For example, *The Night of Nightmares* is a great new DVD.
N: DVD

5. M: *The Night of Nightmares* is a horror movie. And believe me, it really is a very scary movie!

Parents, be careful. This movie is not good for young children.
N: horror

6 M: *Lost in Paris* is a classic romantic movie from Europe. If you like movies about people in love, you have to see it!
N: romantic

7. M: There are all kinds of video cassettes in the movie section. Our store has the largest selection of classic movies on video cassette. *Star Adventure* is a very popular video cassette.
N: video cassette

8. M: *Star Adventure* is an excellent science fiction movie. If you like spaceships and astronauts, you need to see this video.
N: science fiction

9. M: And for book lovers, how about an old-fashioned mystery? *The Stolen Diamond* is one of our bestsellers. Read the book and help the police solve the mystery!
N: mystery

### Pg. 139 Lesson 2—Exercise 3A

Thank you for calling the Multiplex Cinema. To hear movie times, press 1. To hear ticket prices, press 2. To find out about theater locations, press 3. To hear this message again, press 4. To speak to an operator, press 0. Movie times for *Endless Winter* are 5 p.m. and 7:30 p.m. Movie times for *Dangerous Drivers* are 6 p.m. and 8:30 p.m. And finally…

### Pg. 142 Lesson 4—Exercise 1E

W1 = Woman 1, M1 = Man 1, M2 = Man 2, W2 = Woman 2

1. W1: What did you think of that TV show last night?
M1: I thought it was so funny! The best one yet! What did you think?
W1: I thought it was fantastic! I want to see it again!

2. M2: Did you enjoy the concert?
W2: No, I thought it was boring. I nearly fell asleep. What did you think?
M2: I agree. It certainly was bad.

3. W1: How did you like the football game?
M2: It was great! The most exciting game of the season!
W1: Yes, that's true. But I don't like to watch football.

# GRAMMAR CHARTS

## THE SIMPLE PRESENT WITH *WANT TO, LIKE TO, NEED TO*

### Affirmative statements

| | | |
|---|---|---|
| I You | want like need | |
| He She It | wants likes needs | to eat. |
| We You They | want like need | |

### Negative statements

| | | | |
|---|---|---|---|
| I You | don't | want like need | |
| He She It | doesn't | want like need | to eat. |
| We You They | don't | want like need | |

### Contractions

do not = don't
does not = doesn't

### Yes/No questions

| | | | |
|---|---|---|---|
| Do | I you | | |
| Does | he she it | want like need | to eat? |
| Do | we you they | | |

### Short answers

| | | | | | | | |
|---|---|---|---|---|---|---|---|
| Yes, | I you | do. | | No, | I you | don't. | |
| | he she it | does. | | | he she it | doesn't. | |
| | we you they | do. | | | we you they | don't. | |

### Information questions

| | | | | |
|---|---|---|---|---|
| What | do | I you | want | to study? |
| Who | does | he she | like | to visit? |
| How | does | it | like | to eat? |
| Where When Why | do | we you they | need | to work? |

## THE FUTURE WITH *WILL*

### Affirmative statements

| | | |
|---|---|---|
| I You He She It We You They | will | work. |

### Negative statements

| | | |
|---|---|---|
| I You He She It We You They | won't | work. |

### Contractions

I will = I'll
you will = you'll
he will = he'll
she will = she'll
it will = it'll
we will = we'll
they will = they'll

will not = won't

### Yes/No questions

| | | |
|---|---|---|
| Will | I you | |
| | he she it | work? |
| | we you they | |

### Short answers

| | | | | | | |
|---|---|---|---|---|---|---|
| Yes, | I you | will. | No, | I you | won't. | |
| | he she it | | | he she it | | |
| | we you they | | | we you they | | |

### Information questions

| | | | |
|---|---|---|---|
| What | will | I you | study? |
| Who | will | he she | see? |
| How | will | it | work? |
| Where When Why | will | we you they | work? |

## THE SIMPLE PAST

### Affirmative statements

| | | |
|---|---|---|
| I<br>You<br>He<br>She<br>It<br>We<br>You<br>They | liked | the food. |

### Negative statements

| | | | |
|---|---|---|---|
| I<br>You<br>He<br>She<br>It<br>We<br>You<br>They | didn't | like | the food. |

### Contractions

did not = didn't

### Yes/No questions

| | | | |
|---|---|---|---|
| Did | I<br>you<br>he<br>she<br>it<br>we<br>you<br>they | like | the food? |

### Short answers

| | | | | | | |
|---|---|---|---|---|---|---|
| Yes, | I<br>you<br>he<br>she<br>it<br>we<br>you<br>they | did. | No, | I<br>you<br>he<br>she<br>it<br>we<br>you<br>they | didn't. |

### Information questions

| | | | |
|---|---|---|---|
| What<br>How | did | I<br>you | do? |
| Who | did | he<br>she<br>it | see? |
| Where<br>When<br>Why | did | we<br>you<br>they | go? |

### Past tense of irregular verbs

| | | | | |
|---|---|---|---|---|
| be — was/were | drink — drank | hear — heard | put — put | spend — spent |
| become — became | drive — drove | hit — hit | read — read | stand — stood |
| break — broke | eat — ate | hurt — hurt | ride — rode | steal — stole |
| bring — brought | fall — fell | keep — kept | ring — rang | take — took |
| buy — bought | feed — fed | know — knew | run — ran | tell — told |
| catch — caught | feel — felt | leave — left | say — said | think — thought |
| choose — chose | find — found | lend — lent | see — saw | throw — threw |
| come — came | forget — forgot | let — let | sell — sold | understand — understood |
| cost — cost | get — got | lose — lost | send — sent | wake up — woke up |
| cut — cut | give — gave | make — made | sit — sat | wear — wore |
| do — did | go — went | meet — met | sleep — slept | withdraw — withdrew |
| draw — drew | have — had | pay — paid | speak — spoke | write — wrote |

## REASONS WITH *TO* AND *BECAUSE*

### Reasons with *to* + verb

| | | |
|---|---|---|
| Carol used her English book | to study | the new vocabulary. |
| | | grammar charts. |

### Reasons with *because*

| | | |
|---|---|---|
| Kathryn withdrew twenty dollars | because | her son needs money. |
| | | she wants to buy a book. |
| | | she needed money. |
| | | she wanted to eat lunch. |

## THE PAST CONTINUOUS

**Affirmative statements**

| | | |
|---|---|---|
| I | was | |
| You | were | |
| He She It | was | walking. |
| We You They | were | |

**Negative statements**

| | | |
|---|---|---|
| I | wasn't | |
| You | weren't | |
| He She It | wasn't | walking. |
| We You They | weren't | |

**Contractions**

was not = wasn't
were not = weren't

**Yes/No questions**

| | | |
|---|---|---|
| Was | I | |
| Were | you | |
| Was | he she it | walking? |
| Were | we you they | |

**Short answers**

| | | | | | | |
|---|---|---|---|---|---|---|
| Yes, | I | was. | No, | I | wasn't. |
| | you | were. | | you | weren't. |
| | he she it | was. | | he she it | wasn't. |
| | we you they | were. | | we you they | weren't. |

**Information questions**

| | | | |
|---|---|---|---|
| Where | was | I | working last year? |
| Why | were | you | eating cake? |
| Who | was | he she | visiting? |
| When | was | it | raining? |
| What How | were | we you they | doing yesterday? |

| Past continuous | | Simple past |
|---|---|---|
| He was studying | when | the teacher spoke. |
| They were sleeping | | the phone rang. |

## POLITE STATEMENTS AND REQUESTS

**Questions**

| | | |
|---|---|---|
| Can Could | I you he she it we you they | help? |

**Short answers**

| | | | | | |
|---|---|---|---|---|---|
| Yes, | I you he she it we you they | can. could. would. | No, | I you he she it we you they | can't. couldn't. wouldn't. |

## MIGHT, MUST, AND HAVE TO

### Affirmative statements

| | | |
|---|---|---|
| I<br>You | | |
| He<br>She<br>It | might<br>must | sleep. |
| We<br>You<br>They | | |

### Negative statements

| | | |
|---|---|---|
| I<br>You | | |
| He<br>She<br>It | might not<br>must not | sleep. |
| We<br>You<br>They | | |

### Contractions

In the U.S., people don't usually make negative contractions with *might* or *must*.

### Notes

For things that are possible, use *might*.
For things that are necessary, use *must*.

### Yes/No questions

| | | | |
|---|---|---|---|
| Do | I<br>you | | |
| Does | he<br>she<br>it | have to | sleep? |
| Do | we<br>you<br>they | | |

### Notes

In the U.S., people don't usually ask questions with *might* or *must*.
~~Might she sleep?~~
~~Must she sleep?~~

### Short answers

| | | | | | | |
|---|---|---|---|---|---|---|
| Yes, | I<br>you | do. | No, | I<br>you | don't. |
| | he<br>she<br>it | does. | | he<br>she<br>it | doesn't. |
| | we<br>you<br>they | do. | | we<br>you<br>they | don't. |

### Information questions with *have to*

| | | |
|---|---|---|
| How often | does he have to | make photocopies? |
| How many photocopies | | make? |

## PREPOSITIONS

### Prepositions of time

| | | Notes |
|---|---|---|
| I was a student | in 2001. | Use *in* for years and months. |
| | in August. | |
| The class begins | on Monday. | Use *on* for days and dates. |
| | on July 24th. | |
| The movie starts | at 10:45. | Use *at* for times. |
| | at two o'clock. | |
| January is | before February. | |
| December is | after November. | |

# THE COMPARATIVE AND SUPERLATIVE

| | Adjective | Comparative | Superlative | Notes |
|---|---|---|---|---|
| One syllable | small<br>nice<br>hot | smaller<br>nicer<br>hotter | the smallest<br>the nicest<br>the hottest | For comparative, add *-er* or *-r*.<br>For superlative, add *-est* or *-st*.<br>For words like *hot*, double the final consonant. |
| Ending in *-y* | happy<br>noisy | happier<br>noisier | the happiest<br>the noisiest | For comparative, change *y* to *i* and add *-er*.<br>For superlative, change *y* to *i* and add *-est*. |
| Two or more syllables | famous<br>expensive<br>comfortable | more famous<br>more expensive<br>more comfortable | the most famous<br>the most expensive<br>the most comfortable | For comparative, add *more* in front of adjectives.<br>For superlative, add *most* in front of adjectives. |
| Irregular forms | good<br>bad<br>far | better<br>worse<br>farther | the best<br>the worst<br>the farthest | |

| Comparatives in sentences | | | | Notes |
|---|---|---|---|---|
| The computer is | cheaper<br>noisier<br>more expensive<br>better | than | the photocopier. | Use the comparative to talk about two things. |

| Superlatives in sentences | | | Notes |
|---|---|---|---|
| This computer is | (one of) the cheapest<br>(one of) the most popular | of all.<br>in the store.<br>this week. | Use the superlative to talk about three or more things. |

| Questions with *Which* | | Answers |
|---|---|---|
| Which is bigger, | a house or a factory? | A factory is. |
| Which building is bigger, | | A factory is bigger. |

## SENTENCES WITH *TOO*

| *Too* + adjective | | | Notes |
|---|---|---|---|
| It's | too | small.<br>noisy.<br>expensive. | *too* = more than is good<br>Use *too* + adjective. |

| *Too* = also | Notes |
|---|---|
| I'm a student. She's a student, too.<br>I'm a student, and she's a student, too. | *too* = also<br>*Too* comes at the end of a sentence. |

## COUNT NOUNS

| Singular affirmative statements | |
|---|---|
| We have | a cookie. |
| There is | an egg. |

| Singular negative statements | |
|---|---|
| We don't have | a cookie. |
| There isn't | an egg. |

| Plural affirmative statements | |
|---|---|
| We have | two cookies. |
| There are | three eggs. |

| Plural negative statements | |
|---|---|
| We don't have | any cookies. |
| There aren't | any eggs. |

| Singular questions | |
|---|---|
| Do you have | a cookie? |
| | an egg? |

| Answers |
|---|
| Yes, we have a cookie. |
| No, we don't have an egg. |

| Plural questions | | |
|---|---|---|
| Do you have | any | cookies? |
| | | eggs? |

| Answers |
|---|
| Yes, we have some cookies. |
| No, we don't have any eggs. |

| Questions with *How many* | | |
|---|---|---|
| How many | cookies<br>eggs<br>potatoes<br>vegetables<br>carrots | are there? |

| Answers | |
|---|---|
| There is | one cookie.<br>one egg. |
| There are | many potatoes.<br>a lot of vegetables.<br>a few carrots. |

## NONCOUNT NOUNS

| Affirmative statements | |
|---|---|
| We have | some soup.<br>two cans of soup. |
| There is | some soup. |
| There are | two cans of soup. |

| Negative statements | |
|---|---|
| We don't have | any soup. |
| There isn't | much soup. |

| Questions with *How much* | | |
|---|---|---|
| How much | soup<br>ice cream<br>coffee<br>spaghetti | is there? |

| Answers | |
|---|---|
| There is | one can of soup. |
| There are | two cartons of ice cream. |
| There is | a lot of coffee.<br>a little spaghetti. |

# VOCABULARY LIST

# INDEX

## ACADEMIC SKILLS

### Grammar

### Graphs, Charts, Maps

### Listening

## Writing

## CIVICS

## LIFE SKILLS

### Consumer Education

### Environment and the World

### Family and Parenting

### Government and Community Resources

### Health and Nutrition

### Interpersonal Communication